THE STRUGGLE
FOR IDENTITY
IN TODAY'S SCHOOLS

Cultural Recognition in a Time of Increasing Diversity

Edited by
Patrick M. Jenlink and Faye Hicks Townes

Rowman & Littlefield Education
Lanham • New York • Toronto • Plymouth, UK

Published in the United States of America
by Rowman & Littlefield Education
A Division of Rowman & Littlefield Publishers, Inc.
A wholly owned subsidary of The Rowman & Littlefield Publishing Group, Inc.
4501 Forbes Boulevard, Suite 200, Lanham, Maryland 20706
www.rowmaneducation.com

Estover Road
Plymouth PL6 7PY
United Kingdom

British Library Cataloguing in Publication Information Available

Library of Congress Cataloging-in-Publication Data

The struggle for identity in today's schools : cultural recognition in a time of
increasing diversity / edited by Patrick M. Jenlink and Faye Hicks Townes.
    p. cm.
  ISBN 978-1-60709-106-6 (cloth : alk. paper) — ISBN 978-1-60709-107-3
(pbk. : alk. paper) — ISBN 978-1-60709-108-0 (electronic)
  1. Multicultural education—United States. 2. Group identity—United States. 3.
Recognition (Psychology) I. Jenlink, Patrick M. II. Townes, Faye Hicks, 1952–
  LC1099.3.S896 2009
  370.1170973—dc22   2008053372

©™ The paper used in this publication meets the minimum requirements of
American National Standard for Information Sciences—Permanence of
Paper for Printed Library Materials, ANSI/NISO Z39.48-1992.
Manufactured in the United States of America.

This work is dedicated to our mothers—

To my mother, Helen Faye Jenlink, who was there for my first lesson in life and has remained steadfast in her willingness to help me learn, ever the teacher.

To my first teacher, my mother, Mary Lee Hicks, who continuously encourages me through her strength, persistence, and patience.

Contents

Acknowledgements

This volume has been several years in the making. The initial idea for this project began as a conversation focused on recognition and the issue of structure in schooling in an increasingly diverse society. It was Charles Bingham's work *Schools of Recognition: Identity Politics and Classroom Practices* published in 2001 that first stimulated our conversation. Over time, we engaged in related conversations on issues of difference, politics of identity, and culture, always focusing inward on how recognition or misrecognition within sociocultural contexts works to shape and reshape one's identity, whether the student, teacher, or other cultural worker.

Like others before us, we believe that identity is framed by difference, understood not as fact but as perspective. We believe that interwoven with individual identity formation is the development of cultural identity, and how we are recognized or not recognized with the cultural spaces of school and community defines and redefines our identity, as teacher or student or cultural worker.

Equally important, we believe that the structure of schooling and what takes place within the public space of schools today largely influences the shaping of identity. Understanding how recognition and identity come to play on shaping the "self" of a student or teacher, we believe, must be considered within the problematic nature of how schooling is structured and what takes place inside and outside the spaces of classrooms. Like so many scholarly works of this nature, there are many to thank.

First, we wish to thank the authors for not only believing in the idea but also committing to the realization of a volume with diverse perspectives and voices about cultural recognition and the struggle for identity experienced across schools in America. Second, we would like to thank Rowman & Littlefield Education, Tom Koerner, and the editorial staff for their vision in seeing the value of such a work. Also we would like to express our appreciation to Becky Fredrickson, who as a doctoral research assistant invested many hours of editing our words and those of the contributing authors. In addition, we would like to thank Mary Catherine Niño whose work as associate director with the ENLACE Program at Stephen F. Austin brought insightful comments to play in conversations about identity and cultural politics.

Finally, we wish to thank our respective academic units at Stephen F. Austin State University and the College of Charleston for supporting this project and enabling us to realize a work that we believe will further an important and much needed discourse on cultural recognition and the struggle for identity shared by all who are vested in America's schools.

Patrick M. Jenlink, Stephen F. Austin State University
Faye Hicks Townes, Charleston College

Preface

Charles Taylor, in his *Sources of the Self: The Making of the Modern Identity*, published in 1989, and later in an essay titled "The Politics of Recognition," published in 1994, offered a different way of thinking about the public space of school and the structure of schooling. Taylor brought to the foreground what most liberal conceptions do not speak to, the possibility that one's particularity, one's very identity, is itself needy, vulnerable, malleable, and even multiple in public spaces such as the school. Awareness of the sources of self is central to understanding the shaping of identity and the struggles often experienced in forming an identity having one's identity defined by others. It is in understanding the sources of self that we begin to understand the relation that exists between recognition and identity: how one's identity is constructed within social and cultural contexts, as an individual and as a member of different cultural groups.

Following Taylor's work, Charles Bingham, writing in *Schools of Recognition: Identity Politics and Classroom Practices* (2001), focused on recognition theory and shaping of identity in the educational setting. Recognition as identity shaping is concerned with identification, within social, cultural, and political contexts. As sociocultural process, recognition must consider both the constructive nature it has in relation to identity shaping as well as the cultural politics of the recognitive process, that is, how the dominant ideologies of different cultures work to shape one's identity through the recognitive process.

Recognition, or the absence of recognition, or the influence of ideologically charged recognition, gives way to a politics of identity. Identity politics, the tendency to base one's politics on a sense of personal identity, assumes that the most radical, activist politics develop when one comes to understand the dynamics of how one is oppressed and how one oppresses others in his or her daily life.

In large part, educators who understand the formation of students' identities are educators who also understand the formation of their own identities. Whether it is the curriculum that helps students understand that prevailing social practices are the product of Eurocentric cultures or whether it is in the sense that educators, including ethnic minority educators, must learn to examine the consequences that those prevailing social practices have jointly had in the creation of their own lives and the lives of their students. Cultural recognition and the struggle for identity in schools is a *constant* in the ongoing dynamics of a changing America, and in the recognition that difference is a defining element of our identities whether we are educators or students or citizens in our communities.

Recognition, as identity shaping, is situated in social-cultural contexts and is concerned with public space, such as a school. Within this public space, one's particularity, one's very identity, is itself vulnerable, malleable, and even multiple in public spaces such as the school. The recognitive process that an individual experiences within social-cultural contexts is replete with multiple encounters that shape identity, one's own and the identity of others. Such encounters begin with the assumption that neither knowledge nor acknowledgement is ever just ours to decide, that recognition always takes place within a larger horizon of socially imbued discourses, and that those discourses are circumscribed by social power, institutional constraints, and hegemonic norming. Both knowing *about* a person and *confirming* a person need to be considered within the context of the largely unspoken cultural assumptions that inform them.

In this volume, the authors examine cultural recognition and the struggle for identity in America's schools. In particular, the authors focus on the recognition and misrecognition as antagonistic cultural forces that work to shape and, at times, distort identity. Each author brings a unique perspective to his/her examination of cultural recognition as identity shaping within social, cultural, and political contexts.

What surfaces throughout the chapters are two lessons that can be learned in relation to identity. The first lesson is that identities and the acts attributed to them are always forming and reforming in relation to historically specific contexts, and these contexts are political in nature, that is, defined by issues of diversity such as race, ethnicity, language, sexual orientation, gender, and economics. The authors acknowledge that identities and their cultural resources are responses to, develop in, and so are inclusive of the dilemmas fostered by the struggles, personal crises, and social recruitment under which they form.

The second lesson presented by the authors is that identity forms in and across intimate and social contexts, over long periods of time. The historical timing of identity formation cannot simply be dictated by discourse. The identities posited by any particular discourse become important and a part of everyday life based on the intersection of social histories and social actors. Importantly, the social-cultural use of identities leads to another way of conceptualizing histories, personhoods, cultures, and their distributions over social and political groups.

The authors present to the reader an important and continuing critical dialogue on cultural recognition and the struggle for identity, hallmarked by historical, cultural, and political tensions that leave their imprint on the lives of students and teachers, and the larger community served by America's schools. The authors remind us that we (students, teachers, administrators, parents, community leaders) interact in ways that reflect positive or negative views of each other. Regardless of the source of those views, they impact us. As part of the cultural dynamics of the school, these views hurt or help the negotiation of cultural identity and the structure of schooling.

Introduction: Cultural Identity and the Struggle for Recognition

Patrick M. Jenlink and Faye Hicks Townes

Charles Taylor (1989), in *Sources of the Self: The Making of the Modern Identity*, argued that modern identity is characterized by an emphasis on the authenticity of its inner voice and the quest of finding a way of being that is somehow true to oneself. In a postmodern world, it could now be argued that while each individual is capable of animating his or her reason or moral sense to live authentically, the politics of difference has appropriated the language of authenticity to describe ways of living that are true to the identities of marginalized social groups.

If one ponders what matters with respect to an individual's authentic self, much the same as Appiah (2000) does in speaking to racial identity and racial identification, what moves to the foreground is a question of why is much contemporary talk about large collective identity categories that seem so far removed from the individual? What is the relationship between this collective language and the individualistic thrust of the self?

Appiah argues the connection between individual identity and other collective identities—group identity and identification—lies along two dimensions. One is a collective dimension comprising race, gender, ethnicity, nationality, sexuality, and so forth, and the

1

other is a personal dimension, comprising socially or morally important dispositions. The importance of collective identities is evident in that they provide narrative scripts, which shape individuals' life stories and identities and are simultaneously used in telling an individual's life story and writing his or her identity.

Narrative scripts are the medium of identity formation and identification. They are what Kerr (1997) refers to as the circuits of recognition, the points of intersection for personal and collective identities, inside and outside the formal structures of schooling. These points of intersection enable society to mirror or reflect back to individuals how others see the individual through his or her actions and in relation to the groups one is affiliated with, either by choice or the action of an external force.

Recognition and the Formation of Identity

According to Taylor (1994), in an essay titled "The Politics of Recognition," how others recognize us is central to the formation of our identity. How we are seen or recognized by others becomes, negatively or positively, a part of our identity. This form of recognition, or misrecognition, is a form of societal mirroring, which Taylor explains:

> Our identity is partly shaped by recognition or its absence, often by misrecognition of others, and so a person or group of people can suffer real damage, real distortion, if the people or society mirror back to them a confining or demeaning or contemptible picture of themselves. (1994, 25)

In schools individuals (students, teachers, administrators, staff, parents, community leaders) interact in ways that reflect positive or negative views of each other. Cooley (1902), writing in the now classic text, *Human Nature and the Social Order*, referred to this process metaphorically as the looking-glass self, where reference groups and significant others serve as "mirrors" that reflect the images of the self. The basic idea for the looking-glass self is drawn from the couplet quoted by Cooley:

> Each to each a looking glass
> Reflects the other that doth pass. (1902, 152)

Simply stated, we recognize and are recognized through the lens of the "self"; recognition is a mirroring process and the person serving as our mirror—our looking glass—is of crucial importance in the process of self-definition: defining and redefining one's identity. Regardless of the source of those views, they impact us.

Schools of Recognition—Understanding the Mirror

Furthering the ideas of self and identity and recognition set forth in the work of Taylor (1989, 1994), Charles Bingham (2001), in his *Schools of Recognition: Identity Politics and Classroom Practices*, presents the question: "What role might recognition play in education?" (3). In this work, he emphasizes recognition as it occurs in the social and cultural space of schools. As part of the cultural dynamics of schools, Bingham argues that examining recognition—the social mirroring—is necessary to understanding how individuals—students, teachers, parents, other cultural workers and vested individuals—negotiate the structures of schooling.

In a public setting such as school, we encounter instances of recognition. Recognition, at its simplistic level, is "the act of acknowledging others, and coming to be acknowledged by others" (Bingham, 2001, 3). Exploration of the intricacies imbedded in the act of recognition, however, reveals the cultural norms that are at work. We bring to the act of recognition our preconceived notions about the roles that others play, or should play, in our lives and in society. When we participate in the act of recognition, we, in many ways, help to shape the people we recognize, the structure wherein the recognition takes place, and the society in which we live.

As the public school system becomes more and more diverse, relationships inherent in its structure (student-to-student, teacher-to-teacher, administrator-to-teacher, school boards-to-administrators, parent-to-teacher, etc.) also become more complex. Bringing together a myriad of political affiliations, sexual orientations, economic levels, belief systems, and cultural norms, the institution of schooling is ripe with opportunities for encounters with recognition.

In light of the importance of and the abundance of recognitive occurrences in the public school setting, Bingham's (2001) proposal for a discourse of recognition for educators is a point well taken. As we search for that discourse, we should be aware that the search, discovery, and use of this discourse of recognition, while rewarding, might also be a challenging and even painful journey.

Discourses of Recognition—Understanding the Forces at Work

Discourses of recognition, from the perspective of student groups who typically see themselves as marginalized in a school setting, provide a viable medium for understanding recognition in relation to formation of identity. As an example, marginalization, a force at work in student groups, is often exemplified by groups with status problems by "external forces that mark a group of people as a distinct segment from the rest of the population" (Ogbu, 2004, 4). Within the social and cultural contexts of schools, groups perceived as having and/or groups experiencing status problems may include, but not be limited to, students with disabilities; lesbian, gay and bisexual (LGB) students; racial, ethnic, and language minority students; or low SES students. Whether this marginalization is real or perceived, it can have a negative impact on the school experiences of students.

As human beings, we want to belong, to feel accepted. Students want to belong when it comes to their schools. They want to be mirrored positively in their interpersonal encounters in the public place of school. As Bingham (2001) explains, "When I enter the public sphere, I need someone, or something, that will mirror back to me an affirming sense of who I am" (34). In this sense, the mirror of recognition—the looking-glass self—not only reflects the one looking into the mirror, it also constitutes the individual; it defines the individual's identity. This interprets as identity being far less static than one might imagine.

Furthering Cooley's (1902) looking-glass self metaphor and Bingham's (2001) mirror metaphor, Gloria Anzaldúa (1990) draws attention to the politics of identity when she writes:

> "Making faces" is my metaphor for constructing one's identity
> . . . In our self-reflectivity and in our active participation with the

issues that confront us, whether it be through writing, front-line activism, or individual self-development, we are also uncovering the inter-faces, the very spaces and places where our multiple surfaced, colored, racially gendered bodies intersect and inter-connect. (xvi)

Identity, as portrayed in Anzaldúa's metaphor, articulates an awareness that instead of being limited to steadfast representations of *who I am*, identity needs to be embraced by *who I turn out to be* in relation to the ideological and political imprints in the social and cultural contexts within which identity is defined and redefined. This means for students and teachers that what must be considered is not only the structural, but the political, curricular, and interpersonal practices that work to shape individuals' identity, but also how these practices can lead to the misrecognition and malrecognition of students.

If we examine, through recognitive lenses, what we teach and how we teach, as well as how we interact socially and subjectively, on the pedagogical and curricular practices and how they impact all students, we will find ourselves moving outside ideological boundaries that all too often work to marginalize and otherwise subordinate students as "others," not like us, or different. If we understand how our students are mirrored in the structures of schooling—the curricular, political, epistemological, pedagogical, and so on—it can become a basis for transformative social change.

However, one cannot address a problem or issue until one acknowledges that a problem exists. A discourse of recognition is a way to illuminate injustices that have thrived under the guise or protected cover of tradition and organizational structure. As Bingham (2001) notes:

> Both the larger cultural critiques of recognition and the more specific educational critiques remind us that a struggle focusing solely on positive recognition is a struggle that ignores a large part of human reality. Recognition has its downsides, both in the public sphere at large and . . . in educational spaces. (343)

A discourse of recognition is also important to identifying and addressing the problematic nature of misrecognition or malrecognition, born of ideological and/or political imprints of culture and society and emblematic of racism, genderism, sexism, classism, and related forms of marginalization and oppression experienced in America's schools.

The Struggle for Identity in Today's Schools—
At a Glance

In the chapters that follow, the reader will join with the contributing authors in a series of conversations that attempt to illuminate the meaning and nature of recognition as it relates to defining and redefining identity in the social, cultural, and historical context of schooling in America. The authors, through their respective perspectives, examine cultural recognition and the struggle experienced daily by teachers and students and other cultural workers in America's schools. The authors illuminate many of the often problematic structures of schooling and the cultural politics that work to define one's identity. *The Struggle for Identity in Today's Schools* is organized into two parts.

In the part I, Cultural Identity—Toward a Politics of Identity (chapters 1, 2, and 3), the authors present three perspectives that examine the politics of recognition and identity and the cultural work of educators in America's schools. In chapter 1 an examination of identity politics, recognition, and the cultural work of schools is presented, illuminating the complex relationship of identity and recognition. Chapter 2 presents a dialogue on racialized identity and the necessary steps toward a politics of recognition, engaging the reader in an examination of the historical 1954 Brown v. Board of Education juxtaposed to current court decisions, and the unfolding of a politics of recognition concerned with racialized identity. Chapter 3 examines the concept of misrecognition, arguing that examining policies and practices in our schools through the lens of recognition can help illuminate our treatment of difference.

Part II, Struggle for Recognition—Embracing Cultural Politics (chapters 4–13), presents a set of perspectives on cultural identity and the role recognition in the structure of schooling. Here, the authors examine the antagonistic relationship between recognition and misrecognition, juxtaposed with such issues as centered on

English-language learners, Asian American students, curriculum, fine arts, sports, parental involvement, preparing students for post-secondary education, diversity and difficult conversations, and community.

At the heart of each chapter, the authors focus on the importance of understanding recognition as a critical factor in shaping identity, not just for students but also for teachers and others who work in schools are shaped by the ideological and political patterns of culture and dominance. The closing chapter offers the reader considerations for recognition, difference, and the future of America's schools.

Closing Thoughts

A discourse of recognition makes different claims about the nature of self and identity than does a discourse of tolerance. The self, as exemplified in a theory of recognition, is not autonomously situated. Instead, the self always looks to others for its sense of identity: it looks to the "mirror," the "looking-glass self" that reflects what others, what society sees us as, and at the same it shapes and constitutes our identity. The importance of the "mirror" that defines and redefines identity lies in understanding that experiencing the other is as important as knowledge of the other, and that interpersonal confirmation is fundamental to recognition in the structures of schooling. Critical to realizing schools of recognition is the cultivation of discourses that enable individuals to illuminate and interrogate cultural and political and pedagogical patterns and practices that translate into teaching and learning that fosters formation of identity and recognition: affirming the identity of the student or the teacher or the other, thus enabling the individual to flourish and mature into a productive American citizen.

References

Anzaldúa, G. (1990). *Making face making soul/Haciendo Caras: Creative and critical perspectives by feminists of color*. San Francisco: Aunt Lute Foundation Books.

Appiah, K. A. (2000). Racial identity and racial identification. In L. Back & J. Solomon (Eds.), *Theories of race and racism: A reader* (607–15). London: Routledge.

Bingham, C. W. (2001). *Schools of recognition: Identity politics and classroom practices.* Lanham, MD: Rowman & Littlefield.

Cooley, C. H. (1902). *Human nature and the social order.* New York: Charles Scribner's Sons.

Kerr, D. (1997). Toward a democratic rhetoric of schooling. In J. I. Goodlad & T. J. McMannon (Eds.), *The public purpose of education and schooling* (73–83). San Francisco, CA: Jossey-Bass.

Ogbu, J. (2004). Collective Identity and the burden of "acting white" in Black history, community, and education. *Urban Review, 36*(1), 1–35.

Taylor, C. (1989). *Sources of the self: The making of the modern identity.* Cambridge, MA: Harvard University Press.

Taylor, C. (1994). The politics of recognition. In A. Gutman (Ed.), *Multiculturalism: Examining the politics of recognition* (25–73). Princeton, NJ: Princeton University Press.

I

CULTURAL IDENTITY—
TOWARD A POLITICS
OF IDENTITY

1

Cultural Identity—Toward a Politics of Identity

Identity is something that co-emerges with one's ever-shifting geographical, interpersonal, and intertextual experiences, and that identity is always the product of the interpretative work done around the continual fusing of past, present, and projected senses of self.

Sumara, 1998, 206

The self is the place from which persons view or sense the world and reflect upon it. There is no presumption that a person has only one important sense of self, or an impetus to consistency across these different senses of self . . . the selves . . . are assembled from, and in relation to cultural resources.

Holland, 1998, 289

Identity is not static or disembodied; rather it varies by time, place, and interactions according to specific social situations and within differing cultural contexts. An individual who defines him- or herself in a certain way in one context may don a different defining identity in another context. Defining oneself in relation to one's cultural and social community also defines one's participation within that community, both one's connection and affiliation as well as one's responsibility. One's identity is further defined when one claims that one is *of* the group (that is, chooses to affiliate one's self or is placed by others within a particular group—Puerto Rican, African American, Asian American, Hispanic, Jewish, Catholic, Protestant, male, female, disabled, bisexual, etc.).

Cultural identity is often framed by difference, understood not as fact but as perspective. "What is not" defines the boundaries of "what is." Who is the same as I am, who is other, and according to what criteria? How are racial differences essential or constructed, and what do they mean in our lives? Educators and students live in a world where difference connotes not equal, better (worse), having more (less) power over resources. Discourses of identity and difference are interwoven at many points with a discourse of racism, genderism, and sexism; both the interpersonal and the structural (Cohen, 1993).

Interwoven with individual identity formation is the development of cultural identity, in our society closely linked with racial identity and ethnic identity. Strong and complex identification with one's culture and community are necessary not only for survival, but also for a positive sense of self and for the making of an involved and active community member (Helms, 1990).

Constructing cultural identities in a culture-biased society is a demanding task, one in which the structure of schooling plays a key role, particularly if we recognize that equality of treatment does not guarantee equality of opportunity. Education that invites teachers and students and other cultural workers to construct cultural knowledge should affirm all lived experiences (Cohen, 1993). In addition to all teachers and students consistent participation (or nonparticipation) in their cultural community of origin, it is also important to understand that their cultural identity and predominant bicultural responses are also influenced by their efforts to contend with the social tensions that are inherent in conditions of cultural subordination. As a consequence, individuals from subordinate groups must interact within society and schooling structures that consistently produce varying levels of cultural conflict and dissonance. Their responses to the power differential and to their consequent inferior social status play an important role in the development of bicultural identity (Darder, 1995).

Therein lies the importance of discovering and developing one's own authentic voice linked with the discovery and articulation of one's own identity (Taylor, 1991), the development of a sense of efficacy, of personal dignity and worth. This means uncovering both for ourselves as educators and cultural workers as well as for our students "the deep structural factors which have a tendency persistently not only to generate racial practices and structures but to reproduce them through time which therefore account for their extraordinarily immovable character" (Hall, 1981, 61).

References

Cohen, J. (1993). Constructing race at an urban high school: In their minds, their mouths, their hearts. In L. Weis & M. Fine (Eds.), *Beyond silenced voices: Class, race, and gender in United States schools* (289–308). Albany: State University of New York Press.

Darder, A. (1995). Buscando America: The contribution of critical Latino educators to the academic development and empowerment of Latino students in the U.S. In C. E. Sleeter & P. L. McLaren (Eds.), *Multicultural education, critical pedagogy, and the politics of difference* (319–47). Albany: State University of New York.

Hall, S. (1981). Teaching race. In A. Jones & R. Jeffcoate (Eds.), *The school in multicultural society* (59–69). London: Harper & Row.

Helms, J. (1990). *Black and white racial identity*. New York: Greenwood Press.

Holland, D. (1998). *Identity and agency in cultural worlds*. Cambridge, MA: Harvard University Press.

Sumara, D. J. (1998). Fictionalizing acts: Reading and the making of identity. *Theory into practice*, 37(3), 203–10.

Taylor, C. (1991). *Sources of self*. Cambridge, MA: Harvard University Press.

1

Affirming Diversity, Politics of Recognition, and the Cultural Work of Schools

Patrick M. Jenlink

As teachers and leaders in America's schools, we live in a world articulated and predicated on difference, a world in which affirming diversity and developing multicultural educational environments present complex political and pedagogical challenges. Giroux (1991) helps us to understand that difference, in this sense, "is not about merely registering or asserting spatial, racial, ethnic or cultural difference, but about historical differences that manifest themselves in public and pedagogical struggles" (516). At issue for America, as for much of the world, is the concern for how we will live with our deepest differences. More important, central to this concern is addressing the kind of difference that is acknowledged and engaged, rather than simply acknowledging difference exists.

Jay (1991) is instructive when he explains that who we are as a society, our commonality, "is not a substance of essence (Americanness)," but rather it is "a process of social existence predicated on the espoused if not always realized principles of cultural democracy, political rights, community responsibility, social justice, equality of opportunity, and individual freedom" (265). When we fail to affirm our diversity, that is, when the principles of cultural democracy "are subordinated to totalizing ideologies seeking to invent or impose a common culture, the actual multicultural life of Americans suffers under oppression that is in no one's best interests" (Jay, 1991, 266).

Affirming of Diversity—Making the "Other" Visible

The affirmation of diversity is concerned with cultural and social invisibility; it is an issue of social justice and democracy. Policies and practices that work to affirm diversity translate, in part, as a commitment to making the "Other" visible, committing to creating a space for the Other. As Dolby (2000) explains, "Difference is inscribed as a space of authenticity—a place where real selves reside and are waiting to be discovered" (907). This is a space made authentic through the practice of multicultural education where all students are visible to the teacher and to society.

In schools and classrooms, teachers are confronted with invisibility as a moral and social issue. The narrator in Ralph Ellison's (1952) *Invisible Man* is instructive in helping us to understand invisibility:

> I am an invisible man. No, I am not a spook like those who haunted Edgar Allen Poe; nor am I one of your Hollywood-movie ectoplasms. I am a man of substance, flesh and bone, fiber and liquids—and I might even be said to possess a mind. I am invisible, understand, simply because people refuse to see me. . . . When they approach me they see only my surroundings, themselves, or figments of their imagination—indeed, everything and anything except me. . . . That invisibility to which I refer occurs because of a peculiar disposition of the eyes of those with whom I come in contact. A matter of the construction of their inner eyes, those eyes with which they look through their physical eyes upon reality. (7)

Rather, it is understood as a phenomenon of society's inner eyes constructed through a variety of factors, some ideological, others economic and social, and some simply racist. But at the heart of the issue is a realization that these inner eyes are constructed by an absence of imagination—the absence of an ability to see the invisible as living human beings, as persons, like all other persons. Nieto (2004) observes in this regard: "Our society, among many others, categorizes people according to both visible and invisible traits, uses such classifications to deduce fixed behavioral and mental traits, and then applies policies and practices that jeopardize some and benefit others" (36), the inner eyes of society fail to see that which is different.

However, it is not only those who can look right through individuals as if they didn't exist; the individuals themselves come to doubt if they exist:

> You wonder whether you aren't simply a phantom in other people's minds. Say a figure in a nightmare, which a sleeper tries with all his strength to destroy. . . . You ache with the need to convince yourself that you do exist in the real world, that you're a part of all the sound and anguish, and you strike out with your fists, you curse and you swear to make them recognize you. Alas, it's seldom successful. (Ellison, 1952, 7–8)

Ellison's novel concerns marginalization, a refusal of acknowledgment, a humanity that has been effaced. Marginality and effacement suggests invisibility. From its very opening, however, the novel itself goes to work deconstructing that refusal of recognition, making the Other visible, alluding as it does so to its own moral capacities (Nussbaum, 2002).

Transforming the invisible means transforming the inner eyes of society, thus making visible those individuals and groups marginalized and oppressed. Such transformation may best be accomplished by education as function of a multicultural democratic society; transformation that begins with teacher education that is multicultural and affirming of differences that define individual identity.

In preparing students for their role in a society defined by diversity—ethnic, racial, cultural, linguistic, gender, sexual orientation, and so on—educators must embrace a concern for the problem of invisibility. In so doing, educators must incorporate in the curriculum a quality of vision that enables teachers and students to look imaginatively at the differences of individuals, groups, and society represented by the students who enter teacher-education programs. The type of vision necessary in today's diverse and multicultural societies understands that making the Other visible must necessarily involve making visible those dominant discourses in education that block teachers' and students' fuller potential with respect to understanding their work in building a democratic, multicultural society and in helping marginalized students construct empowering identities.

The Diversity Imperative

At a time when the demographic shifts in society reflect an increasingly diverse population and the dominant political agendas work to redefine the federal government's role in education, it is important to recognize that the new conservative view on education has resulted in a shift away from defining schools as agencies of equity and justice as democratic ideals. Growing calls for accountability and standardization, as Nieto (2004) explains, "have led to eroding attention to equity in education, and teachers are pressured to teach a restricted curriculum to align more closely with the standardized tests that their students must pass" (xviii). There is diminishing concern with how public education could better serve the interests of diverse groups of students by enabling them to understand and gain some control over the sociopolitical forces that influence their destinies.

In the new conservative discourse and its preoccupations with accountability schemes, testing, accreditation, and credentializing, we find school life—teaching and learning—primarily defined by measuring its utility against its contribution to economic growth and cultural uniformity; there is a silent erosion of democratic ideals by this conservative discourse, a new invisibility.

At its center, the diversity imperative is a counternarrative that speaks to linking difference, schooling, and democracy as the work of institutions of public and higher education, acknowledging that schools must educate students primarily for the responsibilities of learning how to be critical, democratic citizens. This means organizing curricula in ways that enable and empower students to examine and make judgments about how society is historically and socially constructed, what has engendered social and cultural invisibility, and how existing social relationships and dominant ideologies structure inequalities around racism, sexism, and other forms of oppression.

It also means preparing teachers who embrace democratic ideals in their practice and who, through their pedagogy, offer students the possibilities for being able to make judgments about what society might be, what is possible or desirable outside existing configurations of power (Darder, 1995; Delpit, 1993; Gay 1997b; Giroux, 1991; Ladson-Billings, 1995).

Politics of Recognition—Identity and Identification in a Diverse Society

At the heart of a politics of recognition is a realization that our society, as Nieto (2004) argues, "categorizes people according to both visible and invisible traits, uses such classifications to deduce fixed behavioral and mental traits, and then applies policies and practices that jeopardize some and benefit others." This form of societal recognition or misrecognition is hallmarked by two major problems: "First, people of all groups begin to believe the stereotypes, and second, both material and psychological resources are doled out accordingly" (36). Such discrimination yields a destructive force that affects the identity/identification of individuals. Far greater is the destructive nature of institutional discrimination guided by policies and practices that a devaluing "effect on groups that share a particular identity (be it racial, ethnic, gender, or other)" (37).

The politics in the "the politics of recognition" speaks to the use or misuse of power that results in discrimination, marginalization, and subordination of some individuals, often those who are defined by their differences. The major distinction "between individual and institutional discrimination is the wielding of power, because it is primarily through the power of the people who control institutions such as schools that oppressive policies and practices are reinforced and legitimated" (Nieto, 2004, 37).

At issue for educators in schools today, as for much of the world, are two simple but profound questions that run through education: How will we live with our deepest differences? How will those differences be used by others to determine an individual's identity? These questions bring to the foreground a concern for the politics of recognition; the forming of individual identity and the identification of an individual with different cultural groups. In constructing an identity, one draws, in part, on the difference in people available in one's society (Appiah, 2005).

Students, teachers, and other cultural workers in schools have multiple "identities, constructed across different, often intersecting and antagonistic, discourses, practices and positions. They are subject to a radical historicization, and are constantly in the process of change and transformation" (Hall, 1990, 34). Because these multiple, social identities are constructed within, not outside, discourses of recognition (or misrecognition), we need to understand them as constructed in specific historical and institutional contexts within specific discursive formations and practices, by specific ideological embedded enunciative strategies (Hall).

Charles Taylor (1994), in his essay, "The Politics of Recognition," argues that the lack of political recognition of ethno-cultural minority identities represents a core problem for minorities. This argument can be extended to other issues of difference including religious, class, and sexual orientation. The politics of recognition is concerned with identity, which reflects a deep ethical problem that predisposes it to demand deference to claims phrased in the language of group identity and experience (McBride, 2005). Connolly (2002) is instructive in understanding the politics of recognition:

> An identity is established in relation to a series of differences that have become socially recognized. These differences are essential to its being. If they did not coexist as differences, it would not exist in its distinctness and solidity. Entrenched in this indispensable relation is a second set of tendencies, themselves in need of exploration, to conceal established identities into fixed forms, thought and lived as if their structure expressed the true order of things. When these pressures prevail, the maintenance of one identity (or field of identities) involves the conversion of some differences into otherness, into evil, or one of its numerous surrogates. Identity requires differences in order to be, and it converts difference into otherness in order to secure its own self-certainty. (64)

Individuals are shaped through the intersubjective process of recognition, in which the individual's identity is formed through a dialogic process whereby the individual comes to recognize him or herself in the other. In this sense, recognition refers to the ways in which the act of recognition constitutes the object of recognition (Honneth, 1996; Taylor, 1994).

Struggling for Recognition

Recognition is not a single act. Struggles for recognition strive not only to protect otherwise neglected minorities, they are also a form of discourse on the social meaning of our moral and political standards. As Taylor (1994) explains, "Our identity is partly shaped by recognition or its absence, often by misrecognition of others" (25). Within schools today, in the classrooms the ubiquity and importance of the struggle for recognition is undeniable, whether in the form of the struggle of the immigrant to be recognized as someone who "belongs," or the struggles of students to be recognized for their differences as valuable members of the class and society.

Arguably, the problem of escaping oppressive forms of social recognition is typically one of liberation from particular forms of "recognition" (forms such as dominate and dominating discourses ideologically inscribed in the cultural and structures of schooling, or forms such as racism, genderism, sexism, etc.), a process that demands the critical scrutiny of social relations and in the attempt to transform these relations, the withholding of recognition from those aspects of social identities implicated in inequality (McBride, 2005).

Withholding Recognition

Educators and other social workers must necessarily examine the structures of schooling and the larger social and cultural contexts within which students live. This means looking at the ideological and political inscriptions in the day-to-day practices of teaching and learning as well as looking outside the walls of classrooms and schools to the overlay of similar inscriptions that dominate where the student lives and learns when away from school.

It is important to realize that it is not enough to understand the politics of recognition; one must act on that understanding: politics of recognition demand that educators take a stance on recognition. Teachers must understand, and help students to understand, that our identity is premised in part on knowing when to give recognition that is formative and affirming, and knowing when to withhold recognition from certain persons or aspects of their self-presentation, we need only reflect upon the complex interaction of social identities. Individual identities are multilayered and hierarchical in relationship to others. "Difference" may itself be a product of inequality. Thus it is not simply the case that identities are constituted by their place within a system of differences, but that these differences themselves are often hierarchical, such that one term is treated as lesser than the other, a deviation or lack and so on (McBride, 2005).

Clarifying Recognition and Misrecognition

Understanding the politics of recognition interprets, in part, as clarifying how the concepts of "recognition" and "misrecognition" can be used in regard to these instances of situated politics of recognition in which conflicting claims of difference and sameness are posed. Misrecognition of social identities means that the agency of a student, taking part in direct social interaction—such as teaching and learning—within the social context of a classroom, is judged by other standards than those normally associated with the context itself.

If the categorical identity of ethnicity or class or sexual orientation comes to be seen as imperative to the social identity associated with the context itself, this social identity is misrecognized. Having one's identity defined by others, assigned an identification to a particular cultural group, strips the individual of voice in determining his or her identity; a form of misrecognition resulting in discrimination, marginalization, or subordination.

Misrecognition of social identities, thus, can be understood as a form of "symbolic violence," through which individuals are made inferior, devalued on the basis of the ascribed to them Otherness. In the case of ethnic minority youth, misrecognition of social identities can be seen if their behavior in interethnic contexts, such as the classroom, marching band, or athletic club, is judged according to assumptions of ethnicity as an imperative identity dimension. In such cases, the categorical identity of ethnicity is given legitimacy as the imperative interpretational frame—how one is identified, and the identities related to the pupil, musician, or athlete statuses are made secondary. Recognition of a social identity, then, takes place when persons are judged with reference to a moral or cultural frame relevant to the activities and practices taking place within this specific context (Andersson, 2004).

The Cultural Work of Schools—An Unfinished Agenda

The transformation of American society into a more just, equitable, inclusive, and critical democracy will depend in large part on the ability of public and higher education to articulate and implement the diversity imperative. Closely related to the diversity question is the ideology question, which asks: "What is the purpose of schooling, what is the role of public education in a democratic society, and what historically has been the role of schooling in maintaining or changing the economic and social structure of society?" (Cochran-Smith, 2003, 11).

Although we live in a multicultural society that claims democratic identity, invisibility remains an endemic problem that must be addressed in preparing educators for the cultural work of schools. It is important to address the problem beginning with educator preparation (and therein teacher and leader educators), who must change not only the program but the "self" of each person responsible for educator preparation; changing "existing ideologies, values, assumptions, and instructional practices undergirding the preparation of teachers as well as its curriculum content" (Gay, 1997a, 159).

Until multiple cultural competencies and critical pedagogical considerations are at the core of educator preparation and professional development, the diversity imperative will remain in the shadows of societal invisibility. The unfinished work lies, in part, in addressing "the ideologies underlying many school policies and practices," which are based on misconceptions of intelligence and difference (Nieto, 2004, xxii).

If educator preparation is to change the situation, it means preparing teachers who will enter schools with an understanding that their work, in large part, is "changing the curriculum and pedagogy in individual classrooms, as well as the school's practices and the societal ideologies supporting them" (Nieto, 2004, xxii). This will require that teacher education also recognize as part of the larger political and pedagogical agenda that "we need to create not only affirming classrooms but also an affirming society in which racism, sexism, social class discrimination, and other biases are no longer acceptable" (xxii).

Unfinished Cultural Work of Schools— Changing Education's stance

Changing traditional education to reflect a cultural of recognition and multicultural education stance on teaching and learning responds to the diversity question and interprets the ideology question in critical, pragmatic terms. The idea of redefining education as multicultural forces us to "recognize our complicity in accepting and perpetuating biases whether it be sexism, racism, or homophobia" (hooks, 1993, 96). As well, it causes us to make visible social boundary lines: "such lines as sexual orientation, gender, class, race, ethnicity, nationality, age, politics" (Rosaldo, 1989, 208) that define individual and group identity, and often narrowly define curriculum and instruction, constraining teaching and learning.

Many schools have been, and continue to be, entirely removed from an imaginative vision and a set of practices dedicated to fostering the diversity imperative, democracy, or social justice. The work ahead for education lies, in part, in examining and responding to the moral implications of societal inequalities within the educational system, and the ways in which schools function to reproduce and legitimate these inequalities. For educator preparation programs in many "institutions, there is enormous inconsistency in faculty members' knowledge, information and depth of understanding about issues related to culture and teaching underserved populations" (Cochran-Smith, 2003, 18).

Understanding the politics of recognition and taking a cultural stance on affirming diversity, as well as a stance on identity formation as a social and moral responsibility of schooling, requires embracing a critical pedagogical approach to teaching. This critical approach will necessarily need to be concerned with a focus on social justice and a discussion of historical and contemporary inequalities. What is common to these approaches is a shared notion of identity and a focus on what identity is as opposed to how it is produced.

In part, the unfinished work of education is to turn inward and look at the current structures of schooling, working to create schools of recognition. Schools of recognition understand the politics of diversity and work to affirm the identity of each individual while simultaneously working to ensure that identification with cultural groups is a choice on the part of the individual and a positive force in developing social identities.

Simply stated, education in schools of recognition is culturally sensitive to political and ideological tensions, necessarily focusing on the centrality of identity in educating students whose identity formation is aligned with ideals of justice, equity, and democracy. Educators who understand the formation of their students' identities are educators who also understand the formation of their own identities (Monteninos, 1995). This means that current dominant patterns (whiteness) that define education are redefined by engaging an imperative for diversity. In this sense, "Teachers, including ethnic minority teachers, must learn to examine the consequences that prevailing social practices have jointly had in the creation of their own lives and the lives of their students" (Monteninos, 1995, 297).

Changing education must focus on multicultural curriculum and culturally responsive pedagogy that helps "teachers uncover how their lives and the lives of their students intertwine" (Monteninos, 1995, 297) and, equally important, how the politics of identity works within and through curricular and pedagogical considerations in both teacher preparation and practice and how visibility can be created and cultured and invisibility eliminated.

Unfinished Cultural Work of Schools—Creating Space for Cultural Invention

Embracing the politics of recognition and the need for multicultural education requires that educators, in creating the space for learning and teaching, recognize that the multiple realities of teaching diverse populations are socially constructed and identity in turn is constructed within this subjective frame of reality. As Harvey (1996) puts it, "Symbolic orderings of space and time provide a framework for experience through which we learn who and what we are in society" (214).

Preparing ourselves as teachers to enter classrooms hallmarked by diversity suggests that we ask: How can we position ourselves as less masters of truth and more as creators of a space in which those directly involved can act and speak on their own behalf? (Lather, 1991). This will require a rethinking of learning that creates what Bhabha (1988) calls a space of negotiation and translation. More important, it requires that we create "space for cultural invention," recognizing that "the weight of subjectivity which goes with" cultural invention, "is not the same as respecting identities which exist and which are endeavoring to maintain their existence, even if the two registers tend constantly to overlap" (Wieviorka, 1998, 907).

Cultural invention as the unfinished cultural work of schools stresses the political nature of cultural tensions "by examining how institutions, knowledge, and social relationships are inscribed in power differently" (Giroux, 1991, 510), recognizing that teaching, which embraces a multicultural and critical pedagogical stance, "highlights the ethical by examining how the shifting relationships of knowing, acting, and subjectivity are constructed in spaces and social relationships based on judgments which demand and frame" (510) responses in degrees of definition to the complex nature of teaching students from multiple cultures.

That is, teacher practice that embodies cultural invention is concerned with undoing invisibility by recognizing Otherness as critical, cultural, and spatial qualities of teaching and learning to work to create diverse, democratic citizens. Cultural invention addresses the absence of imagination in society, undoing the efface-ment of that society, or in particular those members of society historically made invisible.

Unfinished Cultural Work of Schools—Completing the Social Contract of Democracy

The unfinished cultural work of America's schools extends deeply into the social foundations of society. Banks (1997) explains, in matters of creating democratic schools and by extension demo-cratic society, which recognizes that students come from diverse racial, ethnic, and cultural origins, that teachers "must examine their cultural assumptions and attitudes, their behaviors, the knowledge and paradigms on which their pedagogy is based, and the subject-matter knowledge they teach" (99).

The unfinished work for schools, in part, resides in re-creating the culture of schooling as a culture of recognition. It entails, in part, creating multicultural education programs that work to pre-pare teachers as agents of an educational system and students as agents of a democratic way of life, within an increasingly diverse, democratic society. As educators, part of our democratic impera-tive is to "acknowledge and challenge the injustices that pervade our world" (Nelson-Barber & Harrison, 1996, 261). Invisibility is an injustice that continues to pervade American society and the world at large.

Unfortunately, many political decisions today are based on rhetoric that expounds the virtue of a particular state or federal mandate; however, when the mandate is activated, the interpreta-tion in schools falls dramatically short of the promise. Conse-quently, injustices are compounded and individuals and groups are made more invisible as ideological agendas are perpetrated on society: "Students (and educators) have extensive personal experi-ence with these injustices, whether we are victims of, struggle against, or benefit from them" (Nelson-Barber & Harrison, 1996, 261). In effect, the social contract of democracy is further weakened and society's trust is betrayed.

Education as an agency of democracy has a responsibility for ensuring the integrity of the social contract. Gay (1997a) speaks to the importance of multicultural education and how teacher education that is multicultural takes a stance of diversity that is also a recognition of each individual's right to the "social contract of democracy" (2). Teaching, which is concerned with the social contract of democracy, must also be concerned with the diversity imperative in teaching that understands "that neither students in school nor society at large are best served by the way schooling (the social contract of education) is traditionally conceived and practiced." Therefore, the unfinished cultural work of schools, in part, is to renegotiate the "structures and processes of education" through multicultural education "to make them more inclusive of the cultures, experiences, perspectives, and contributions of all ethnic groups that comprise the United States" (2).

Final Reflections

As educators and cultural workers we should never adapt ourselves to another human being's invisibility, nor, more important, contribute to invisibility through our practice. Invisibility continues as one of society's historical legacy and insidious threats. Addressing invisibility, addressing the injustices that pervade society and its educational system, will not be easy work. It will require, as Dewey (1902) states, "travail of thought" (182), and it will require, as Nieto (2004) explains, "challenging racism and other biases as well as the inequitable structures, policies, and practices of schools and, ultimately, of society itself" (xxvii).

Our unfinished work as a democratic society is embracing our increasing diversity and by so doing, embracing our potential as an authentic democracy. Our unfinished work as educators' centers on diversity and the imperative for transforming traditional education schools into schools of recognition and education that is responsive to the cultural diversity that defines our society. What this means is uncertain, and uncertainty creates differing degrees of fear for educators and policy makers and ideologues.

We will need to challenge existing ideologies about education, schooling, and society that conflict with multicultural perspectives of knowledge, practice, and ways of teaching and learning. Equally important, we will need to challenge the politics of diversity and recognition that influence recognition and misrecognition, which in turn shape individual's identity and influence identification within and across multiple cultural groups.

We will need to change the stance that education has taken, traditionally, and affirm diversity as an imperative for preparing teachers for society's classrooms and, equally important, for preparing students to meet the responsibility of an increasingly diverse society. In turn, we will need to create new spaces that enable cultural invention in educator preparation programs and public schools, transforming traditional spaces that render invisible segments of society while maintaining dominance and visibility of select members of society. Foremost, we need to continue the work of democracy, working to renegotiate the social contract in such ways that recognize and are responsive to changing ideologies and creating democratic spaces.

References

Andersson, M. (2004). *The situated politics of recognition, ethnic minority, youth and identity work*. London: University of London.

Appiah, A. K. (2005). *The ethics of identity*. Princeton, NJ: Princeton University Press.

Banks, J. (1997). *Educating citizens in a multicultural society*. New York: Teachers College Press.

Bhabha, H. (1988). The commitment to theory. *Social Formations, 5*, 5–22.

Cochran-Smith, M. (2003). The multiple meanings of multicultural teacher education: A conceptual framework. *Teacher Education Quarterly, 30*(2), 7–26.

Connolly, W. (2002). *Identity\difference: Democratic negotiations of political paradox*. Minneapolis: University of Minnesota Press.

Darder, A. (1995). Buscando America: The contribution of critical Latino educators to the academic development and empowerment of Latino students in the U.S. In C. E. Sleeter & P. L. McLaren (Eds.), *Multicultural education, critical pedagogy, and the politics of difference* (319–47). Albany: State University of New York.

Delpit, L. (1993). The silenced dialogues: Power and pedagogy in educating other people's children. In L. Weis & M. Fine (Eds.), *Beyond silenced voices: Class, race, and gender in United States schools* (119–39). Albany: State University of New York Press.

Dewey, J. (1902). *The child and the curriculum*. Chicago: University of Chicago Press.

Dolby, N. (2000). Changing selves: Multicultural education and the challenge of new identities. *Teachers College Record, 102*(5), 898–912.

Ellison, R. (1952). *Invisible man.* New York: Signet Books.

Gay, G. (1997a). The relationship between multicultural and democratic education. (Special Section: Citizenship Education and Multicultural Education at a Crossroads). *Social Studies, 88*(1), 1–8.

Gay, G. (1997b). Multicultural infusion in teacher education: Foundations and approaches. *Peabody Journal of Education, 72*(1), 150–77.

Giroux, H. (1991). Democracy and the discourse of cultural difference: Towards a politics of border pedagogy. *British Journal of Sociology of Education, 12*(4), 501–19.

Hall, S. (1990). Cultural identity and diaspora. In J. Rutherford (Ed.), *Identity* (222–37). London: Lawrence & Wishart.

Harvey, D. (1996). *Justice, nature & the geography of difference.* Cambridge, MA: Blackwell.

Honneth, A. (1996). *The struggle for recognition.* (Joel Anderson, Trans.). Cambridge, MA: MIT Press.

hooks, b. (1993). Transformative pedagogy and multiculturalism. In T. Perry & J. W. Fraser (Eds.), *Freedom's plow: Teaching in the multicultural classroom* (91–97). New York: Routledge.

Jay, G. (1991). The end of 'American' literature toward a multicultural practice. *College English, 53,* 264–81.

Ladson-Billings, G. (1995). Multicultural teacher education: Research, practice, and policy. In C. A. Banks (Ed.), *Handbook of research on multicultural education* (717–61). New York: Macmillan.

Lather, P. (1991). *Getting smart: Feminist research and pedagogy within the postmodern.* New York: Routledge.

McBride, C. (2005). Deliberative democracy and the politics of recognition. *Political Studies, 53,* 497–515.

Monteninos, C. (1995). Culture as an ongoing dialog: Implications for multicultural teacher education. In C. E. Sleeter & P. L. McLaren (Eds.), *Multicultural education, critical pedagogy, and the politics of difference* (291–308). Albany: State University of New York.

Nelson-Barber, S., & Harrison, M. (1996). Bridging the politics of identity in a multicultural classroom. *Theory into Practice, 35*(4), 256–63.

Nieto, S. (2004). *Affirming diversity: The sociopolitical context of multicultural education* (4th ed.). Boston: Pearson Education.

Nussbaum, M. (2002). Education for citizenship in an era of global connection. *Studies in Philosophy and Education, 21,* 289–303.

Rosaldo, R. (1989). *Culture & truth: The remaking of social analysis.* Boston: Beacon Press.

Taylor, C. (1994). The politics of recognition. In A. Gutman (Ed.), *Multiculturalism: Examining the politics of recognition* (25–73). Princeton, NJ: Princeton University Press.

Wieviorka, M. (1998). Is multiculturalism the solution? *Ethnic and Racial Studies, 21*(5), 881–910.

2

Dialoging Toward a Racialized Identity: A Necessary First Step in a Politics of Recognition

Kris Sloan

In June 2007, the Supreme Court struck down the efforts by two communities (Louisville, Kentucky, and Seattle, Washington) to address school segregation, also described as racial isolation. Chief Justice John Roberts insisted that the Court was remaining faithful to the 1954 Brown v. Board of Education ruling in barring public school districts from assigning students on the basis of race as an effort to address issues of racial isolation and to achieve levels of diversity in schools that reflect the racial diversity of the community as a whole. Moreover, the court majority opined that these communities' *voluntary* school desegregation plans discriminated against a small handful of white students in ways similar to the ways state-sponsored segregation policies had discriminated against black students prior to the Brown decision.

Chief Justice Roberts, along with Justice Clarence Thomas in his own written opinion, suggests that the people Brown was supposed to protect (namely, black students barred from attending schools with whites) were "the same" as the people who this ruling protects (namely, a small group of white students voluntarily asked to attend a school outside of their neighborhoods for the purpose of reducing racial isolation in schools).

The text of the majority ruling opinions is heavily laden with languages and rationales consistent with what Charles Taylor (1994) characterizes as Kantian notions of liberalism, which Walzer (1994) refers to as "liberalism 1." This brand of liberalism, argues Taylor, fails to adequately incorporate the politics of recognition because it ignores the *dialogical*, which I take to mean the *historically situated*, character of human life. Clearly, one of the crucial sites of dialogue for any culture wishing to realize an authentic politics of recognition involves history, or the sociohistorical narratives cultures draw on to tell stories of "now" and "then" (den Heyer, 2003). Below, I return to the importance of sociohistorical narratives as a strategy to help teachers think in more nuanced and complex ways about the ways race shapes the politics of recognition.

To treat or position the black defendants in the 1954 Brown case as "the same" as the white defendants in the latest school desegregation case, the majority of the Supreme Court drew on a signifier—"race"—that bares little historical resemblance to its 1954 form. Columbia Professor Jack Greenberg, who worked on the Brown case for the plaintiffs, characterized as "preposterous" the ways the Justices in the majority deployed the term race in their opinions. Professor Greenberg explained, "The plaintiffs in Brown were concerned with the historical marginalization and subjugation of black people. [The Court in Brown] said you can't consider race, but that's how race was being used (in the 1950s)" (quoted in Liptak, 2007). Professor Greenberg went on to highlight the irony of deploying the term *race* in a way that seems to not only protect privilege for some students but also to thwart expanded opportunities for students who have been historically underserved, even mis-served, by public schools.

By positioning the black defendants in the 1954 Brown case as the same as the white defendants in this latest school desegregation case, by using the term *race* as a mechanism to restrict opportunities for students of color, the Supreme Court also highlighted another tension inherent in modern liberalism that Taylor deftly describes: the tension between the *politics of universalism* and the *politics of difference*. Taylor correctly points out that the politics of universalism, with its emphasis on the "sameness" of all citizens, regardless of race, class, gender, and so forth, tends to work to the advantage of those in dominant categories and to the detriment of those in historically marginalized categories.

The politics of universalism does so because the political mold for such "difference-blind" forms of liberalism is often cast in ways that reflect not only the values, but also the epistemological imperatives of those in the dominant positions. Together, these values and imperatives become potential sources of cultural hegemony that work to marginalize, even alienate, certain groups and undermine the politics of recognition.

Race and the Politics of Universalism

Enacting a politics of universalism tends to lead to a conflation of sameness with equity. In other words, such politics cultivates the belief that to be equal one must be the same—to be treated equitably is to be treated the same. However, feminist and critical race theorists are quick to point out that genuine equity comes not through sameness but through an acknowledgement and recognition of difference. For example, people of color do not have to "be like" whites, dress like white people, speak like whites to be "equal." Equality stems not from being the same, but from being different, yet having (and being recognized as having) equal value.

The difference-blind politics of universalism frequently surfaces in education in the all-too-familiar, liberal "color-blindness" discourse. When issues of race are raised in schools, it is not uncommon for white teachers and administrators alike to insist that they are color blind: that they see children as children, students as students, and they do not see race. Holding tightly to that liberal tenant "skin color shouldn't matter" not only allows whites to dismiss the experiences of people of color, but to ignore their own privilege as whites.

Linda McNeil (2000) argues that current test-based accountability systems undermine the concept of equitable access to education by the acceptance of "sameness" as a standard for equity. Testing systems, McNeil argues, mask educational inequities behind test scores. For example, in the State of Texas a group of Mexican American students who had earned all of their high school credits, but did not pass the state's high school "exit exam," sued the Texas Education Agency because they were denied a high school diploma.[1] In this lawsuit, the students' access to a test score displaced access to an equitable education. The presiding judge used test scores as evidence that the state has "successfully remediated" nearly fifty thousand students who had failed their first attempt on the state high-school exit exam.

The problem with using sameness of tests and of test preparation as a proxy for equity is that this sameness does not carry the same (educational) value. As McNeil states, "The nature of the remediation, the potential losses of subject-matter learning during remediation sessions, and the educational consequences of the remediation were left unexamined (by the court)" (McNeil, 2000, 512).

Race and the Politics of Difference

A listing toward a more dogmatic form of politics of difference has its own set of unique problems, especially in schools. In response to calls for group-based recognition, critical theorists, including race, feminist, queer, and postmodernist theorists have voiced important concerns about an overreliance on a politics of difference. As Baum (2004) cogently points out,

> Claims about supposedly fundamental differences between groups of people, rooted in race, sex, culture, nationality, sexual orientation, and ableness/disability, have been used to justify various forms of intergroup and intragroup oppression between and within societies. (1074)

That is, recognizing or defining people of color as fundamentally "different" from whites has generally left people of color more—not less—vulnerable to white-European cultural norms and values. These norms and values, in the end, not only privilege whites, but constrain what people of color can do or be.

That the problem of addressing the historic academic underachievement by students of color has a tendency to create a listing toward a politics of difference surfaces in the "learning styles" or "multiple intelligences" literature (Frisby, 1993). As most practicing teachers and teacher educators will attest to, the learning style educational literature (see, for example, Dunn and Dunn, 1992; 1993) and Howard Gardner's (1983) theory of multiple intelligences research have proven to be seductive narratives.

In many ways, these bodies of research and scholarship confirmed what most educators intuitively knew: Students have different cognitive strengths and weaknesses, thus they learn new concepts and ideas in different ways. It did not take long, however, for the learning styles or the multiple intelligences discourses to become a source of misrecognition in terms of addressing the learning needs of students of color (Frisby, 1993). I have not only overheard conversations, but also have actively participated in conversations between and among teachers in which black students were positioned as "body-kinesthetic" learners and Latino students as "interpersonal" (or "social") learners. In explaining her room arrangement to me, one white teacher explained, "I sit students together at tables, not individually in desks, because I know that Hispanic kids excel in their interpersonal intelligences."

After such a conversation, I am brought back to Vivian Paley's (1979/2000) seminal book, *White Teacher*. About her own struggles to understand "fears and prejudices, apprehensions and expectations, which have become a carefully hidden part of every one of us" (xx), "The Black child is Every Child. There is no activity useful only for the Black child. There is no manner of speaking or unique approach or special environment required only for Black Children" (xix). That the complexities of the learning styles and multiple intelligences learning theories have been reduced to such a racialized politics of difference, often times essentializing students of color, demonstrates the robust, albeit carefully hidden, nature of race in schools.

Dialoging Toward a Balance

Recognizing the limitations of both the politics of universalism and difference, Taylor proposes an alternative model of liberalism, which Walzer (1994) calls "liberalism 2." This alternative model seeks a balance between the two. Specifically, liberalism 2 works to secure a balance between group rights with individual rights while at the same time recognizing the collective identity-related visions of cultural and social groups. By adding "group claims" to individual claims, Taylor makes clear that there exist collective goals that are not reducible to the universal individual.

To achieve this balance, Taylor draws attention to the dialogical possibilities of human identity. Such possibilities not only open the door to a more productive and inclusive politics of recognition, but they also increase humans' capacity to define themselves and produce self-authored actions that are not oppressive to others. In short, a balance between a politics of universalism and a politics of difference creates the optimal conditions for human agency. In what follows, I link Taylor's thinking about the fundamentally dialogical character of human identity to my own work on issues of identity (formation) and (teacher) agency. Whereas Taylor speaks in general philosophic registers about the possibilities of recognizing and working through the inherent tensions in Western notions of liberalism, I will speak in more specific ways about the ways race plays out for teachers in the cultural politics of recognition. It is my contention that race, or more specifically white racism, has been, is now, and will continue to be the single most intractable impediment to achieving a balance between a politics of universalism and a politics of difference. Indeed, white racism is the most significant impediment to the creation of an inclusive, nonoppressive politics of recognition and to overall improvements in education.

Naming Racism, White Racism

To be sure, there are many variables that contribute to the differential experiences and outcomes among different groups of public schools students. Poverty, family makeup and stability, cultural views of education, school funding mechanisms, class size, and teacher quality all influence the overall quality of students' experiences in schools and their academic outcomes. However, controlling for these variables, race has been, and continues to be, the single most robust predictor in the following negative educational experiences or outcomes:

- Low achievement and poor grades
- Attending primary or secondary schools with larger class sizes
- Dropping out of schools or grade level retention
- Being suspended from school or receiving disciplinary actions for school behaviors
- Attending a more dangerous, less well-funded school
- Limited access to career or academic counseling (Council of Economic Advisors, 1998; United for a Fair Economy, 2004).

Whereas most people acknowledge that the negative educational outcomes listed above are linked to, or associated with, race, few ever attempt to connect them to another important statistic. According to the National Center for Educational Statistics (NCES, 2004), 89 percent of all K–12 teachers in the United States self-identify as white. In all of the talk about the historic problem of the achievement gap between white students and students of color, I find it troubling that the makeup of the teaching force itself has not been offered as one of the possible reasons for the achievement gap. I do not mean to suggest that "the problem" is easily solved by hiring more teachers of color, or that a white teacher cannot successfully teach a student of color, or even that teachers of color would be better for such students than a white teacher.

What these statistics scream out to me is a need for white teachers to come to a clearer understanding of the complexities of racism and of themselves as a racialized identity. Coupling these statistics scream out for the need for white teachers to attend to the multitude of ways race—both consciously and unconsciously—shapes their actions with and beliefs about the children in their classrooms.

Not positioning white racism at the center of the conversation about seemingly intractable problems such as those listed above creates the increased potential for a politics of difference to dominate. A clear example of this can be found in the explanation for the disparate achievement levels between blacks and Mexicans and white college students offered by University of Texas at Austin law professor Lino Graglia: "blacks and Mexicans are not competitive with whites in selective institutions. It is the result primarily of cultural effects. They have a culture that seems not to encourage achievement. Failure is not looked upon with disgrace" (quoted in Foley, 1997).

Graglia's comments offended the sensibilities of Mexican and black families everywhere and reinforced the stereotype that students from communities of color do not value achievement the way whites do. Such remarks are the product of a largely unexamined white supremacist ideology that propagates the insidious belief that whites deserve to be in positions of power because of "merit" and that somehow people of color are to blame for their lot in life.

I now describe a few of my efforts to engage the mostly white preservice teachers in my education classes in explicit conversations about race in general and white racism in particular. My goals include engaging white preservice teachers in sociohistorical narratives about race in ways that provide them with the conceptual tools necessary to work through the complexities of race as they grow into their profession. Although it is important to engage in dialogue with others about ways in which their identities—racial or otherwise—can be recognized, it is perhaps more important for white teachers to first recognize themselves in racialized ways, lest they misrecognize the social, emotional, and learning needs of an ever-expanding population of students of color in their classrooms.

Misrecognizing the Problem

Over a decade ago, Lilia Bartolomé (1994) voiced a concern that much of the current debate—both then and now—concerning the historic underachievement of students of color takes place at a level that treats "the problem" as primarily a technical issue. That is to say, the historical academic underachievement by students of color is most often attributed to faulty or inadequate teaching methods or educational programs. Positioning the problem in such a way means that the only possible solutions to be considered involved the "right" teaching methods or finding the "best practices."

Like Bartolomé, I am continually confronted each semester by eager preservice teachers who are anxious to learn the latest—and greatest—teaching methods. They seem to be crying out for a bag of pedagogic tricks that will magically help them succeed with students with whom other teachers have failed. Such a focus on generic teaching methods, which Bartolomé describes as a "methods fetish," that they think will work with *all* students of color reveals a whole host of other problematic assumptions, assumptions that further undermine teachers' abilities to understand ways they themselves may inadvertently contribute to the historic problem of underachievement by students of color. These assumptions include:

> (1) They, as teachers, are fine and do not need to identify, interrogate, and change their biased beliefs and fragmented views about subordinated students; (2) schools, as institutions, are basically fair and democratic sites where all students are provided with similar, if not equal, treatment and learning conditions; (3) children who experience academic difficulties (especially those from culturally and linguistically low-status groups) require some form of "special" instruction since they obviously have not been able to succeed under "regular" or "normal" instructional conditions. (174)

One of the greatest challenges facing me as a teacher and educator has been helping white preservice teachers to understand that a myopic focus on teaching techniques will, in the end, undermine their abilities to equitably address the needs of their future students.

What I Mean by Racism

I most often begin an extended journey through race and racism with the following statement: "If you are a white person who has grown up in North American, you are a racist." I quickly add, by "racist" I do not mean to suggest that every white person expresses overtly racist ideologies concerning the inherent inferiority of people of color and supports practices and groups that reflect that belief. By racist I am talking about the fact that racism lurks deep in the heart and psyches as a result of being raised in a society based on a white supremacist ideology. I suggest it is impossible to find a white person who has not been, in one way or another, affected by this aspect of the American society.

Drawing on a framework describing various "levels" of racism developed by James Scheurich and Michelle Young (1997), I attempt to help preservice teachers understand that racism is both broader and deeper than overt, individual exhibitions of racism. As John Ogbu (1978) pointed out in the late 1970s, racism in the United States is overwhelmingly seen as an individual phenomenon. This all too easily allows a typical person who is mostly committed to an antiracist's personal stance to state: "I'm not racist, I don't approve of people who are." However, Scheurich and Young point out that positioning "the problem" exclusively at the individual level serves as a "barrier to a broader, more comprehensive understanding of racism" (5).

To broaden and deepen preservice teachers understanding of racism, I present examples of institutional racism, societal racism, and civilizational (or ideological) racism, and finally epistemological racism. As we explore these other levels of racism, I go to great lengths to emphasize that although individual acts of racism may be hurtful, far greater damage is done to peoples of color through institutional, societal, ideological, and epistemological racism. It is through these deeper and broader levels of racism that economic and political powers and practices are channeled through institutions (including schools) to the detriment of people of color.

The "I" Before the "Thou" Before the "It"

To reframe the conversation about the historic underachievement of students of color more tightly around issues of white racism, I begin with a unit of study called "The 'I' Before the 'Thou' Before the 'It.'" The "It" in this case involves teaching methodologies, even techniques. The "Thou" refers to the student and involves the development of skills that help teachers better understand the unique strengths and needs of each student and student group. The "I," of course, involves a process of autobiographical self-study with regard to the ways their past experiences have shaped and continue to shape their lives. It is through autobiographical self-study that I work to tap the dialogical potentials of the human character as described by Taylor.

Invariably in my initial conversations with white preservice teachers about their own identities and their own cultural positions, they are mostly silent on issues of race. In an opening identity-focused activity, I ask the students to write a list of cultural descriptors or markers in response to the prompt: "What/Who are you?" Unlike the preservice teachers of color, remarkably few white preservice teachers include race or "white" in their list of cultural markers. While white preservice teachers may list their ethnic heritage (such as German, French, or Irish), they rarely describe themselves as white. Again, this stands in stark contrast to the preservice teachers of color in my courses. Invariably, these preservice teachers' list of self-descriptors includes racial markers such as "African American," "black," "Mexican American," and "Filipino."

I draw on this opening activity to initiate a conversation about the importance of acknowledging a white racial identity. As Katz and Ivey (1977) state, "Being unaware of one's racial identity and being unable to conceptualize the larger system of 'whiteness' provides a barrier that encases white people so that they are unable to experience themselves and their culture as it really is" (485). Ultimately, this lack of consciousness among white people about their racial identities has two grave consequences. First, it denies white people the experience of seeing themselves as benefiting from racism. Second, it frees them from taking responsibility for eradicating it (McIntyre, 1997; Wellman, 1993).

I follow this activity with an activity that demonstrates one of the ways dominance, even hegemony, perpetuates itself. In their groundbreaking film, *Tough Guise: Violence, Media & the Crisis in Masculinity*, authors, activists, and filmmakers Sut Jhally and Jackson Katz (1999) maintain that the chief means by which dominant, hegemonic perspectives in society remain unchallenged is through invisibility. To make their point, they provide a deceptively simple set of prompts; prompts that I use with preservice when talking to them about the difficulties of identifying sources (not symptoms) of oppression.

- When I say "race," what do you think of first?
- When I say "sexual orientation," what do you think of first?
- When I say "gender," what do you think of first?

Invariably, the first responses for the prompt "race" include Hispanic, African American, and Asian. Their first responses for "sexual orientation" include gay, homosexual, and bisexual. The first response to the prompt "gender," among both women and men, is most often female. As I publicly tally their responses on the white board at the front of the room, many in the room notice a disturbing trend, especially given the racial makeup of the class. In each of the categories provided, the preservice teachers are surprised to discover that they are far quicker to identify marginalized, even subordinated groups, than to identify the dominant group: white, heterosexual, males.

This simple yet powerful activity serves as a bridge to an important conversation about the aims and goals of multicultural education. When asked who multicultural education is "for," most students respond that multicultural education applies to or is for the benefit of "others," but not whites.

After these introductory activities, the more serious and important work begins on helping preservice teachers develop an understanding of themselves as a racialized identity. In his work, Taylor correctly identifies a growing awareness of the dialogical character of human identity. Such an increased awareness holds a tremendous amount of potential to increase humans' capacity, indeed agency, to define ourselves and produce self-authored actions. As I state above, one of the crucial sites of dialogue for any individual involves the sociohistorical narratives he/she draws on to tell stories of "now" and "then." I now move strategies to help teachers think in more nuanced and complex ways about race in general and their own sociohistorical racialized identities in particular.

Teacher Identity and the Politics of Recognition

Through his dialogical perspective of human agency, Bakhtin (1981) asserts that human behaviors are mediated through a continuous process of self-fashioning an "I," or an identity. Put most simply, "People tell others who they are, but even more important, they tell themselves and then try to act as though they are who they say they are" (Holland, Lachicotte, Skinner, & Cain, 1998, 3). Because these processes of self-authoring, or telling others who we are, take place through and around specific social and cultural systems, people develop situative identities—such as "daughter," "mom," "wife," "council member," and "teacher"—by which they are identified and identify themselves. In the context of my own research and this book project, I focus on teachers' teacher identity to better understand the ways they experience and respond to issues of race and culture.

That preservice teachers and in-service teachers develop teacher identities distinctive from those that they self-author in other contexts of their lives is the result of their active participation in the socially produced, culturally constructed context called "school." Holland and colleagues (1998) refer to such contexts as "figured worlds" (41). Figured worlds, in the words of these authors, are

> 1) Historical phenomena to which we are recruited or into which we enter, which themselves develop through the works of their participants . . . (2) social encounters in which participants' positions matter . . . (3) socially organized and reproduced . . . and (4) distribute "us," not only by relating actors to landscapes of actions (as personae) and spreading our senses of self across many different fields of activity, but also by giving the landscape human voice and tone. (41)

Like the other figured worlds described by Holland and colleagues, such as the worlds of romance, therapy, the expected life path of women in Nepal, or Alcoholics Anonymous, "school" for preservice teachers in my courses is not so much a thing or a place, but a complex web of histories, knowledges, processes, and rituals. And it is precisely through the living of this complex web called "school" that teachers (and students) become at once social products *and* social producers.

As social producers, then, teachers (and students) read—consciously or unconsciously—the racialized narratives surrounding them, construct their own unique understandings, and, in the end, construct their own self-directed responses to such narratives. As such, teachers have the potential to be active agents who critically appropriate the artifacts and narratives of race and produce self-authored actions that are more equitable and inclusive (Holland et al., 1998). Although agency in area of race may indeed be frail, Holland and colleagues remind us that "[agency] happens daily and mundanely, and it deserves our attention" (5).

To help preservice teachers explore their budding teacher identities, I ask each teacher to construct a brief school-life narrative related to their own schooling experiences and life as a student. By examining issues of *teacher identity* and identity formation as a base from which to explore *teacher agency* in relation to race, I have found that teacher-identity narratives are powerful means through which to understand their varied experiences with and responses to race.

Merit or Privilege

After the students produce a brief school-life narrative, they share them with a small group of classmates. Discussions of these narratives invariably lead through issues of individual merit and whether schools are set up to reward individuals based on merit alone. This discussion typically moves to questions of whether or not the United States is, or has historically been, a "meritocracy" (McNamee & Miller, 2004). To develop a more critical view of the United States as a meritocracy, I have students read life stories of others. In his book, *The Heart of Whiteness: Confronting Race, Racism, and White Privilege*, Robert Jensen (2005) offers two different stories about himself and asks the reader to judge for herself which one is "true."

In the first story, Jensen reports that he was born in a small town in the Midwest, to parents in the lower-middle class. He reports that he was always expected to work and from the time he started shoveling snow as a child to his current professional career he "worked hard." He studied hard and took school seriously. Jensen worked as a journalist and eventually went back to earn his doctorate and now he is a tenured professor at a major university.

In the second story about himself, Jensen (2005) adds race. He was the child of white, lower-middle-class parents and grew up in a small Midwest town that was almost entirely white. It was white, says Jensen, "because the indigenous population that once lived there was either exterminated or pushed onto reservations" (23). Townspeople liked to joke that the cold winters in his hometown "kept the riff-raff out." The assumption was that "riff-raff" applied not only to those not willing to work hard, but people of color. He went to an all-white school where his accomplishments were applauded and linked to a long line of accomplishments of people who looked just like him.

Jensen's (2005) study of history consisted of knowing about the "victories" and "triumphs" of people that looked like him. He reports attending mostly white colleges where nearly all of his professors were white. In every job he ever had, he was interviewed by a white person. He concludes the second story about himself with this: "I have made many mistakes in my life. But to the best of my knowledge, when I have screwed up in my school or work life, no one has ever suggested that my failures were in any way connected to my being White" (24).

Of course, both of these stories are true, but Jensen wonders whether whites reading it can or are able to recognize the truth in both of the stories. For whites to acknowledge that in addition to all of their effort and hard work, their accomplishments were aided significantly by white privilege involves challenging a powerful American narrative: the American Dream (McNamee & Miller, 2004). This ideological narrative tells Americans that individuals can go as far as their own merit takes them. In the words of Beverly Tatum (1992), "An understanding of racism as a system of advantage presents a serious challenge to the notion of the United States as a just society where rewards are based solely on one's merits" (6).

The notion of white privilege unsettles most whites. It opens the door to difficult questions such as: Do I really deserve my successes? Did white privilege have more to do with my successes than brains and hard work? White privilege, like any social phenomenon, is complex. Although white privilege plays out differently for different people depending on context and other aspects of one's identity, all whites experience some sort of privilege in some settings. Whether they want to or not, whites benefit in a society whose founding is based in an ideology of the inherent superiority of white Europeans over peoples of color.

After discussing the issue of white privilege, I ask students to return to their school-life narratives and to more explicitly talk about race. They then share their stories with their classmates. These narratives are not handed in or graded. It is not my expectation that their newly racialized narratives and the follow-up discussions will help the white students "get it" once and for all. For those who had never even heard of, or even considered, the topics of white racism or white privilege, these conversations are unsettling.

Not surprisingly, the content and discussions can provoke resistance and anger among students. I end the "I" portion of "The I Before the Thou Before the It" unit of study with this idea: We define ourselves, our identities by the stories we tell. The labels and terms we use to tell these stories, what they mean and the ways they apply (or don't) to you or others will always involve a struggle. Understanding the complex ways race shaped our pasts and continues to shape our futures, the ways that race influences our beliefs about others is a life-long process.

The story about how we make meaning of race in general and whiteness in particular is a story that never ends. The histories of inequality and privilege are filled with rhetorical roadblocks and language-game detours that obscure attempts to properly interrogate them. The ultimate goal, for me, is helping preservice teachers to engage in sociohistorical dialogue about race and their own racialized identity in ways that leaves the doors open to future self-study, even self-examination.

Conclusion

As I wrote above, Chief Justice Roberts insisted that the Supreme Court had remained faithful to the 1954 Brown v. Board of Education ruling when it recently barred two public school districts from assigning students on the basis of race as an effort to address issues of racial isolation and to achieve levels of diversity in schools that reflect the racial diversity of the community as a whole. In his majority opinion, Chief Justice Roberts wrote, "The way to stop discrimination on the basis of race is to stop discriminating on the basis of race." In the minority opinion, Justice Anthony Kennedy characterized Chief Justice Roberts as too dismissive of the legitimate interest government has in ensuring all people have equal opportunity regardless of their race and concludes, "While a color-blind Constitution is an aspiration, in the real world, where race often matters, color blindness cannot be a universal constitutional principle."

The achievement of a more authentic politics of recognition, posits Charles Taylor (1994), rests on culture's ability to reach a balance between a politics of universalism and a politics of difference. To achieve this balance, Taylor draws attention to the dialogical possibilities of human identity. Whereas Taylor speaks in broad, philosophical languages about the possibilities of recognizing and working through the inherent tensions in Western notions of liberalism, I offered more specifics about the ways race plays out for teachers in the cultural politics of recognition. In doing so, it is my hope that these strategies not only open the door to a more productive and inclusive politics of recognition in schools and classrooms, but they also increase these preservice teachers' capacity to produce self-authored actions that are not oppressive to others.

Above all, I believe Taylor offers a philosophical framework for ways to tap into the fundamentally dialogical character of human identity in attempt to understand one of this current historical moment's most difficult aspects of the politics of recognition: race.

Note

1. GI Forum et al. v. Texas Education Agency et al., 2000. Also, see the special issue of the *Hispanic Journal of Behavioral Sciences*, 22(4) (November 2000) for a complete description of the case and analysis of the court's ruling.

References

Bakhtin, M. (1981). *The dialogic imagination: Four essays by M. M. Bakhtin*. Michael E. Holquist (Ed.). Caryl Emerson & Michael Holquist (Trans.). Austin: University of Texas Press.

Bartolomé, L. (1994). Beyond the methods fetish: Toward a humanizing pedagogy. *Harvard Educational Review, 64*(2), 173–94.

Baum, B. (2004). Feminist politics of recognition. *Journal of Women in Culture and Society, 29*(4), 1073–102.

Council of Economic Advisers. (1998). Changing America: Indicators of social and economic well-being by race and Hispanic origin. Washington: Author.

den Heyer, K. (2003). Historical agency for social changes: Something more than "symbolic" empowerment. In L. Allen (Ed.), *Curriculum and pedagogy for peace and sustainability* (39–58). Troy, NY: Educator's International Press.

Dunn, R., & Dunn, K. (1992). *Teaching elementary students through their individual learning styles: Practical approaches for grades 3–6*. Boston: Allyn & Bacon.

Dunn, R., & Dunn, K. (1993). *Teaching secondary students through their individual learning styles: Practical approaches for grades 7–12*. Boston: Allyn & Bacon.

Foley, N. (1997). *Reflexiones 1997: New directions in Mexican American studies*. Austin: University of Texas at Austin.

Frisby, C. L. (1993). One giant step backward: Myths of black learning styles. *School Psychology Review, 22*(2), 535–57.

Gardner, H. (1983). *Frames of mind: The theory of multiple intelligences*. New York: Harper & Row.

Holland, D., Lachicotte, W., Skinner, D., & Cain, C. (1998). *Identity and agency in cultural worlds*. Cambridge, MA: Harvard University Press.

Jensen, R. (2005). *The heart of whiteness: Confronting race, racism, and white privilege*. San Francisco: City Lights.

Jhally, S., & Katz, J. (1999). *Tough guise: Violence, media, and the crisis in masculinity*. Northampton, MA: Media Education Foundation.

Katz, J., & Ivey, A. (1977). White awareness: The frontier of racism awareness training. *Personnel and Guidance Journal, 55*(8), 485–89.

Liptak, A. (2007, June 29). The same words, but differing views. *New York Times*, Late Edition, p. A24.

McIntyre, A. (1997). *Making meaning of whiteness: Exploring racial identity with white teachers*. Albany: State University of New York Press.

McNamee, S. J., & Miller, R. K., Jr. (2004). *The meritocracy myth*. New York: Rowman & Littlefield.

McNeil, L. A. (2000). Sameness, bureaucracy, and the myth of educational equity: The TAAS System of Testing in Texas Public Schools. *Hispanic Journal of Behavioral Sciences, 22*(4), 508–23.

National Center for Educational Statistics (NCES). (2004). *Schools and staffing survey (SASS)*. Washington, DC: Institute of Education Sciences, U.S. Department of Education. Retrieved May 23, 2007, from http://nces.ed.gov/surveys/sass/

Ogbu, J. (1978). *Minority education and caste: The American system in cross-cultural perspective.* New York: Academy Press.

Paley, V. (1979/2000). *White teacher.* Cambridge, MA: Harvard University Press.

Scheurich, J. J., & Young, M. D. (1997). Coloring epistemologies: Are our research epistemologies racially biased? *Educational Researcher, 26*(4), 4–16.

Tatum, B. D. (1992). Talking about race, learning about racism: An application of racial identity development theory in the classroom. *Harvard Educational Review, 62*(1), 6–16.

Taylor, C. (1994). The politics of recognition. In A. Gutman (Ed.), *Multiculturalism: Examining the politics of recognition* (25–74). Princeton, NJ: Princeton University Press.

United for a Fair Economy. (2004). The state of the Dream, 2004: Enduring disparities in black and white. Boston: Author.

Walzer, M. (1994). Comment. In Amy Gutman's (Ed.), *Multiculturalism: Examining the politics of recognition* (99–104). Princeton, NJ: Princeton University Press.

Wellman, D. (1993). *Portraits of white racism* (2nd Ed.). New York: Cambridge University Press.

3

Misrecognition Compounded

Faye Hicks Townes

According to Bingham (2001), "Questions of recognition are essential to education" (3). Bingham takes recognition to mean the act of acknowledging others and coming to be acknowledged by others. Under the general category or act of recognition, there is nonrecognition (finding no affirmation during the encounter) and malrecognition (being acknowledged in a way that affronts one's dignity or does not jibe or agree with one's self-image).

As our public schools become more and more culturally diverse, and our classroom teachers become more and more homogenized, attention to multicultural education becomes more pressing. Examining policies and practices in our schools through the lens of recognition can help illuminate our treatment of difference. This illumination is important because when difference is treated negatively in the school setting, the impact reverberates from the individual student to society as a whole (Nieto, 2000).

The need for recognition in the public sphere, in this case the school, is very important because how we are seen and recognized by others, negatively or positively, becomes a part of our identity. According to Bingham (2001),

> With Taylor's historical argument for the importance of public ac-
> knowledgement in mind, one way to describe the event of public
> recognition in schools is to speak in terms of mirrors. That is to say,
> when I enter the public sphere, I need someone, or some thing, that
> will mirror back to me an affirming sense of who I am. (34)

Bingham (2001) further categorizes public recognition or mirroring in the school setting as curricular and interpersonal. Curricular mirroring concerns who is represented in the curriculum of
the school. I would also venture to say that how one is represented
in the curriculum via texts and other written material, the amount
of representation, and teachers' presentation of the material as well
are paramount. If, as a student, I am exposed through the curriculum to negative, distorted, or demeaning views of my culture or
gender, I might prefer that the curricular representation be absent.
Similarly, should my textbook present a representative token mention of my culture or gender, or my teacher hurriedly glosses over
the section that represents me, the reflection, though existent,
would be marred. Being reflected in the curriculum is more than
just text.

Interpersonal mirroring, according to Bingham (2001), "refers
to the fleshly encounter" or when "I can 'see' myself in another's
eyes." In schools students have fleshly encounters almost constantly with other students, teachers, staff, and administrators. The
setting is ripe with opportunities for negative and positive mirroring through interactions. Reports of instances of bullying, violence,
sexual abuse, and other traumatic events in schools attest to the
fact that there are fleshly encounters in schools that do great harm
to students. On the other hand, there are also instances of teachers,
students, and school staff who have gone the extra mile to help students. I, and I am sure many others, have had teachers who provided encouragement and praise at just the right time, and
classmates who made you feel wanted and accepted.

Curricular mirroring and interpersonal mirroring have positive
and negative possibilities. To take a closer, more in-depth view of
curricular and interpersonal mirroring in the realm of schools, I
have revisited data from a previous study of African American females in a majority white high school (Hicks Townes, 1996). In the
study, *Sustaining the Hope: African American Women's Perceptions of*

High School Experiences, the participants were sophomores and juniors from working-class and low-income backgrounds.

Curricular Mirroring

Initially, the juniors in this study came to this majority white school as transfer students. They were recruited to come to the school for a special math and science program that encouraged minority students to enter the field of engineering. Although recruited to come to Singer High School, the black females still experienced marginalization; "To be in the margin is to be part of the whole but outside of the main body" (hooks, 1984, ix). In a school setting, this marginality takes on a slightly different tone. Sinclair and Ghory (1987) define being marginal as "to experience a strained, difficult relationship with educational conditions that have been organized to promote learning" (13). The marginalization experienced by the juniors was academic and social. How could or might this academic and social marginalization experienced by the juniors be viewed through the lens of recognition? Bingham (2001) proposes three qualities of recognition:

> (1) A person can be recognized; that is, one can gain acknowledgement that contributes to one's sense of self, and which affirms one's dignity. (2) A person can encounter nonrecognition; that is to say, one may find no affirmation. In this case, a person does not "find oneself" during the encounter with the other. (3) A person can suffer malrecognition in the sense that one is acknowledged in a way that affronts his or her dignity, or in a way that does not jibe with one's own image of self. The latter two types, nonrecognition and malrecognition, I will lump under the general category of misrecognition . . . Misrecognition, whether it be through absence of acknowledgement, through negative acknowledgement, or through wrong acknowledgement, is an affront to personal dignity. Misrecognition is the undesirable alternative to recognition. (3)

Viewed through the lens of recognition, the academic and social marginalization that the young women experienced comes under the heading of what Bingham refers to as misrecognition (2001).

According to Taylor (1994), how others recognize us plays a role in the formation of our identity. Therefore, how we are seen or recognized by others becomes, negatively or positively, a part of our identity.

Curricular Nonrecognition

Academically the participants were marginalized through the curriculum. They felt that their culture was not addressed in the curriculum and that teachers ignored their concerns and attributes. Their concerns centered on the lack of recognition of Black History Month and their desire for a Black History class. The students did not see their culture or history reflected in the curriculum. As one participant, Elizabeth, stated: "We might have one program out of that whole month. And like we sit in class and listen about white people all the time. In U.S. history it's all you heard." When we consider this exclusion from the curriculum in the context of public mirroring, the impact on the student is obvious; "Who hears his or her story in places such as schools can be crucial to whose dignity is sustained in the larger cultural arena" (Bingham, 2001, 36).

Curricular marginalization and exclusion experienced by the students has a negative and limiting effect. When the dominant culture controls curriculum, it leaves little or no space for the expression of "other" cultures. The marginalized students are limited in their immersion in the school community. They are tolerated as far as presence, but excluded from real participation. Having found no affirmation in the school, the participants experienced nonrecognition. Responding to the curricular nonrecognition they experienced, the participants became advocates for change. They approached their English teachers and asked that they include something for Black History Month in class. Though they had minimal success, it was important that they make the effort. They explained:

> We approached the teacher to say are we going to do something for Black History month? She said yea. And we only did one thing. And that was little; it wasn't much. And to me it was like, oh well, it's over. Might as well not do it. You know but it was that

important to me. I did want to do it. At least we did something. But it ain't enough. It's not enough. (Hicks Townes, 1996)

It is certainly understandable that the participants sought affirmation. The lack of acknowledgement for Black History Month was an indication to the participants that the school did not care about its black students. As they explained:

Think . . . more about the majority of African American kids. Because to me, like Black History month came around and we didn't do anything. And they should, like, take that into consideration. You know, hey, this is important to some of our black youth that goes here. Instead . . . they just didn't do nothing, they just basically did nothing. (Hicks Townes, 1996)

Interpersonal Curricular Nonrecognition

Although Bingham separates the textual from the fleshly encounter, I see the nonrecognition of students in the classroom as a part of curricular mirroring. This is because of the inherent exclusion of perspectives, thoughts, and ideas from the educational conversation when students are ignored. The curriculum cannot effectively reflect the needs and attributes of students who have not been heard. This kind of invisibility in the classroom sends the message that all students are not valued. Participants expressed concern that talents and abilities of black students were not recognized in the classroom. One explained:

Sometimes I feel that I'm treated differently because maybe they don't think I can do as well. But I think I have proved myself pretty much in those situations, because a lot of times I'm the one that comes out and says what's right or . . . just helps another person. (Hicks Townes, 1996)

Another participant was also concerned that teachers at Singer ignore the attributes and needs of black students. She thinks that black students, who can do well academically, don't "and it's because here they don't give you much credit" (Hicks Townes, 1996). Nonrecognition in the classroom can deprive individual students of the help they need and students in general of the wealth of insight and knowledge to be gained from peers.

Extracurricular or Social Nonrecognition

Although extracurricular activities function as nonacademic entities of the school, they do reinforce academic standards (deMarrais & LeCompte, 1999) and reflect the dominant culture of the school. I include the social and extracurricular aspects of the school in this discussion of curricular mirroring for those two reasons. First, when students are culturally omitted from the extracurricular or social aspects of the school, nonrecognition exists. Socially the participants felt distanced from the main fabric of the school. They spoke of being excluded or limited in social or extracurricular activities. The young women also did not see themselves reflected in the social dimension of the school. Second, this nonrecognition of them was also nonrecognition of their culture. Elizabeth, one of the participants, gives an example of this nonrecognition when she talks about representation on the cheerleading squad. She says that the cheerleading situation "is rigged anyway . . . because they pick thin people to be cheerleaders and so you don't have no chance for black people to do anything" (Hicks Townes, 1996). Elizabeth also spoke of having a mixed or biracial cheerleader serving as a black representative on the squad.

> Now last year we didn't have none, because this girl was mixed. They considered her to be black even though she put white on her record. So they made her our black cheerleader. And she don't even consider herself to be black. If you ask her, she'll say she is white. (Hicks Townes, 1996)

Another participant voiced her concerns:

> I mean it was white girl, I mean one black girl. I mean I don't even know if you ought to consider her black. . . . She black on the outside and white on the inside. . . . She got a white boyfriend and everything. . . . She don't conversate with us. (Hicks Townes, 1996)

The participants obviously did not see the "mixed" student on the cheerleading squad as representative of their culture. Elizabeth clearly felt that the physical attributes required to become a cheerleader reflected the values of the dominant culture and not hers. It is interesting to note that Elizabeth did not try to conform to the ideal presented. She did not see her body image as negative. According to Choate (2007), African American girls as a group are less likely to possess negative body image than are other girls. Rather than accept that, she sought to create a way to have her cultural norms affirmed. According to Schooler, Ward, Merriweather, and Caruthers (2004) Black women believe that beauty has more to do with style or character and not the traditional defining aspects of beauty such as appearance and weight. Elizabeth's solution was to start a dance squad that would provide a place for her body image. She related the results of that endeavor.

> So the night we was going to perform, one of the guys had told the cheerleaders that they wasn't letting us. . . . Well, it is one teacher here. . . . And they was saying, the cheerleaders were starting to make fun of us. Like ain't going to have no fun tonight and all this little kind of stuff. So then, they was telling us that we had to pay to get in, and we was to leave. So it turned out that we didn't get to perform. They put us out basically is what you want to say. This lady threatened to call the cops on us if we didn't leave. But the teacher that I say is racist, he turned the lights out on us. (Hicks Townes, 1996)

Again, efforts for cultural affirmation within the school community were unsuccessful. As the school's extracurricular activities reinforce academic standards, they also reinforce the curricular and interpersonal nonrecognition mirrored in the educational practices. The need for positive recognition in the public sphere, in this case the school, is important. The young women did not see themselves (via their culture) reflected in the curriculum, in the classroom, or the extracurricular activities. According to Ladson-Billings (1995) the curriculum should reflect the diversity of social international relationships. Bingham (2001) acknowledges the importance of a curriculum that positively reflects the cultural diversity of our society because "who hears his or her story in places such as schools can be crucial to whose dignity is sustained in the larger cultural arena" (36).

Interpersonal Mirroring

Moving to what Bingham (2001) terms as the "fleshly encounter" on a personal level is more difficult. Perhaps because of this knowledge, I can see elements of hope when simply being ignored: Maybe they just didn't hear me or see me. I can open a discussion that does not exist. I can force the issue. Opportunity exists until proven nonexistent. With the fleshly encounter, more specifically, when it falls into the category of malrecognition, the pain seems more immediate and intense. Bingham (2006) describes this aspect of recognition as occurring when someone is acknowledged in a way that is contradictory to the person's self-image or in a way that affronts his or her dignity. The participants in this study suffered malrecognition from the students, staff, and teachers in the school.

Student Interpersonal Mirroring

When I asked the participants about racial issues at the school, instances of verbal abuse punctuated their stories. Janet talked of being "kicked out cause this girl, she had called me a name and I didn't appreciate, that N word, that she had called me, and so we got into it" (Hicks Townes, 1996). Debra told of a fight that happened when "this one white boy called a black boy an empty-headed nigger and so they started fighting" (Hicks Townes, 1996). The use of the word *nigger* occurred in print as well as speech. Michelle related an experience that caused her to feel anger:

> Like um, confederate stuff. They'll wear that and they'll wear KKK. I've seen someone with a shirt on that had the word nigger on it. And I didn't, I mean, it didn't really bother me at first. I mean, I looked at it, and the rest of the day, it's like, you know, you see people all day. I was just tripping, I mean, cause, maybe that's not a good word but, you know, I don't know, because nobody said anything to him. I'm sure people saw it, because it was

real easy to see, but nobody said anything to him. It's just, they just do stuff like that. (Hicks Townes, 1996)

Essed (1991) explains why a white person calling a black person "nigger" draws a strong reaction from black men and black women:

> U.S. women see racist slurs in a structural context. From that point of view nigger is not a word but a concept representing the history of oppression of Blacks. Name calling then is intimidation because Whites use, as a symbolic weapon, the body of cultural and structural oppression. (256)

It is interesting to note that in the instances of verbal abuse, the black students avoided punishment only when they did not exhibit a response. At least one that was visible.

Faculty Interpersonal Mirroring

Participant interactions with teachers were filled with negative cultural stereotypes. One incident involved stereotypes of black students who have beepers. According to Janet:

> And a teacher asked me the other day, what do you do? You sell drugs? She say what do you do in your spare time? I said work. She said work where? She said do you do . . . illegal stuff? I was like, what do you mean? If you trying to say I sell drugs then you stupid. She said well you don't have to get upset. . . . She said why you got a beeper? I said so my momma can get in touch with me. She said where you be all the time? I said where you be all the time? And she got a beeper, so I said what you doing with a beeper? She said well I work, don't you see? I said what you do in your spare time? And she got upset. (Hicks Townes, 1996)

Janet understood the racism implicit in the questions asked by her teacher. As she states: "They think every black person gotta beeper sell drugs" (Hicks Townes, 1996). Janet saw herself as a student who works and tries to stay in touch with her mother. If she looked into her teacher's eyes she would see herself mirrored as a drug dealer. Participants also spoke of teachers who said that low-income students "won't go to college and they won't graduate" (Hicks Townes, 1996).

The interpersonal mirroring in the participants' encounters with faculty would most certainly be classified as malrecognition. It is most certainly an affront to their dignity and it is out of sync with how the participants see themselves. What must it be like for an adolescent to struggle with this malrecognition on a daily basis? Bingham (2006), in a response to the debate on the recognitive paradigm, says the following:

> In society at large, how people are represented by others will always be a matter of importance, a matter of human dignity. The ways teachers recognize students, the ways students recognize other students, and the ways students are recognized through curricular depictions—these avenues for fostering student dignity are not likely to diminish in importance any time soon. Certainly as the twenty-first century begins, recognition is not about to become less important to human beings. (343)

My experiences as a student, teacher, and human being validate his position. Perhaps awareness of and sensitivity to the importance of recognition is a result of being a woman of color as a student, teacher, and professor in the context of majority white institutions. In these settings, I came (and still come) face-to-face with concerns about the prospect of encountering misrecognition or malrecognition. With years of experience and a thickening of my skin, feelings of dread are balanced with the anticipation of meeting and conquering challenges.

Students from varying ethnic and social groups also continue to face the prospect of misrecognition in the public space of schools. The impact will be felt individually and generally in our society. When students are mirrored an affirming sense of who they are in the school setting, they feel as if they belong. This personal sense of belonging benefits not just the individual student but society in general. According to Wald and Losen (2007):

> The U.S. Surgeon General's report on Youth Violence, released in January 2001, found that "commitment to school" was one of only two buffers against specific risk factors for violence. Another report released in 2002 found that "school connectedness"—

defined as a student's feeling part of and cared for at school—is linked with lower levels of substance use, violence, suicide attempts, pregnancy, and emotional distress. (34)

We, as educators, must rise to the challenge of (1) examining what we mirror to our students, and (2) doing what is necessary to provide affirming recognition through positive mirroring.

References

Bingham, C. (2001). *Schools of recognition: Identity politics and classroom practices.* New York: Rowman & Littlefield.

Bingham, C. (2006). Before recognition, and after: The educational critique. *Educational Theory, 56*(3), 325–44.

Choate, L. (2007). Counseling adolescent girls for body image resilience: Strategies for school counselors. *Professional School Counseling, 10*(3), 317–26.

deMarrais, K. B., & LeCompte, M. D. (1999). *The way schools work: A sociological analysis of education* (Third ed.). New York: Addison Wesley Longman.

Essed, P. (1991). *Understanding everyday racism: An interdisciplinary theory.* Newbury Park, CA: Sage Publications.

Hicks Townes, F. (1996). *Sustaining the hope: African American women's perceptions of high school experiences.* Unpublished doctoral dissertation, University of Tennessee, Knoxville.

hooks, b. (1984). *Feminist theory from margin to center.* Boston: South End Press.

Ladson-Billings, G. (1995). Challenging customs, canons, and content: Developing relevant curriculum for diversity. In Carl A. Grant (Ed.), *Educating for diversity: An anthology of multicultural voices* (327–40). Boston: Allyn & Bacon.

Nieto, S. (2000). *Affirming diversity: The sociopolitical context of multicultural education.* (Third ed.). New York: Addison Wesley Longman.

Schooler, D., Ward, M., Merriweather, A., & Caruthers, A. (2004). Who's that girl: Television's role in the body image development of young white and black women. *Psychology of Women Quarterly, 28,* 38–47.

Sinclair, R. L., & Ghory, W. J. (1987). *Reaching marginal students: A primary concern for school renewal.* Berkeley, CA: McCutchan Publishing Corporation.

Taylor, C. (1994). The politics of recognition. In Amy Gutman (Ed.), *Multiculturalism: Examining the politics of recognition* (25–73). Princeton, NJ: Princeton University Press.

Wald J., & Losen, D. (2007). Out of sight: The journey through the school-to-prison pipeline. In Sue Books (Ed.), *Invisible children in the society and its schools*, Third Ed. (23–37). Mahwah, NJ: Lawrence Erlbaum Associates.

II

THE STRUGGLE FOR RECOGNITION—EMBRACING CULTURAL POLITICS

II

The Struggle for Recognition— Embracing Cultural Politics

You wonder whether you aren't simply a phantom in other people's minds. Say a figure in a nightmare which a sleeper tries with all his strength to destroy. It's when you feel like this, out of resentment, you begin to bump people back. And, let me confess, you feel that way most of the time. You ache with the need to convince yourself that you do exist in the real world, that you're a part of all the sound and anguish, and you strike out with your fists, you curse and you swear to make them recognize you. Alas, it's seldom successful.

Ellison, 1952, 4

If we accept the poststructuralist insight that identity, like language itself, becomes intelligible because it repeats cultural scripts that have already been repeated in the past, then one's horizon is already circumscribed by the historical discourses that are already available.

Bingham, 2001, 97

The struggle for recognition is struggle all individuals are drawn into, and for which all individuals share a responsibility in identifying the ideological and political forces at play in social and cultural contexts. Embracing cultural politics works to mediate the ideological positioning of identity, and it creates discourses within the classroom experiences and structures of schooling that address the difficulty of developing an identity as teacher or student or other. The struggle for recognition does not discriminate; it affects all and it requires us to understand that "even under best of circumstances, even though it might be uncomfortable for us and such a discussion might mean revealing some of our own perceived weaknesses" it is necessary to embrace the politics of culture that work to define and redefine identity (Alsup, 2006, 7).

Individuals live and flourish with what Donna Kerr (1997) has called "circuits of recognition" (73), or they become invisible to society by absence of recognition or as a result of misrecognition when these circuits or recognition do not exist, or exit only for some but not for all. Ralph Ellison's *Invisible Man* (1952) is instructive in understanding the struggle for recognition. Ellison's narrator explains that invisibility "occurs because of a peculiar disposition of the eyes of those with whom I come in contact. A matter of the construction of their *inner* eyes, those eyes with which they look through their physical eyes upon reality" (3). It must be granted that these peculiar inner eyes are constructed through a variety of factors, some economic, social, and ideological, and some simply racist. But at root they are constructed by an absence of imagination—the absence of an ability to see the narrator as a living human being, a man like all other men.

The politics of recognition—an undercurrent of the struggle for recognition—are fundamental in the establishment of trust: individuals will not have confidence in educators or schools or educational institutions if they believe that their values and way of life are not recognized and respected. If individuals do not have trust, they will not learn. A corollary of this principle is that such recognition and respect be accorded within the institution to all participants by all participants. The politics of recognition concern us with identification and the defining of identity.

The struggle for recognition is at the same time social and political work of identification, the defining of one's identity in cultural context. Holland (1998) reveals two interrelated themes at the heart of understanding the struggle: "First, identities and the acts attributed to them are always forming and re-forming in relation to historically specific contexts" (284). Identities and their cultural resources are responses to, develop in, and so are inclusive of the dilemmas by the struggles, personal crises, and social recruitment under which they form.

The second lesson is that identities form situated in intimate and social contexts over long periods of time. The historical timing of this work cannot simply be dictated by discourse. "The conjuncture of the allied personal and social histories . . . determines whether the identities posited by any particular discourse become important and a part of everyday life" (Holland, 1998, 285). Recognition and the struggle for cultural identity are bound in discourses of "identity politics." From this perspective, "identity" is understood as "not only a historical and social construction, but also a part of a continual process of transformation and change" (Giroux, 1992, 172).

Addressing the struggle for recognition in schools across America presents educators and other cultural workers with the challenge to examine and understand the cultural subtexts that imprint ideological and political patterns on the identity of students. With this challenge also comes a corollary challenge to examine, critically, the circuits of recognition at play in the structures of schooling, and to transform the practices and politics that shape identity.

References

Alsup, J. (2006). *Teacher identity discourses: Negotiating personal and professional spaces*. Mahwah, NJ: Lawrence Erlbaum Associates.

Bingham, C. W. (2001). *Schools of recognition: Identity politics and classroom practices*. Lanham, MD: Rowman & Littlefield.

Ellison, R. (1952). *Invisible man*. New York: Signet Books.

Giroux, H. (1992). *Border crossings: Cultural workers and the politics of education*. New York: Routledge.

Holland, D. (1998). *Identity and agency in cultural worlds*. Cambridge, MA: Harvard University Press.

Kerr, D. (1997). Toward a democratic rhetoric of schooling. In J. I. Goodlad & T. J. McMannon (Eds.), *The public purpose of education and schooling* (73–83). San Francisco: Jossey-Bass.

4

Recognition, Identity Politics, and English-Language Learners

Angela Crespo Cozart

For over a hundred years, the Statue of Liberty and its inscription, "Give me your huddled masses . . ." have been the equivalent of America's Welcome mat for newcomers, immigrants like those described in colonial writer J. H. de Crevecoeur's *Letters from an American Farmer:*

> What then is the American, this new man? . . . He is an American, who leaving behind him all his ancient prejudices and manners, receives new ones from the new mode of his life he has embraced, the new government he obeys, and the new rank he holds. He becomes an American by being received in the broad lap of our great *alma mater.* Here individuals of all nations are melted into a new race of men, whose labors and posterity will one day cause great changes in the world. (de Crevecoeur, 1997, 44)

de Crevecoeur saw part of America's greatness stemming from individuals melting into a "new race of men." While immigrants have often been welcomed and encouraged to come to America, at times American citizens have also shown crass disregard and outright hatred for newly arrived immigrants. In order to understand how immigrants forge new identities, it is important to look into

America's contradictory immigration laws and its collective feelings toward new arrivals, especially those who do not speak English. How people are received and viewed by those around them is important in the development of their identities.

Norton posits that identity "refer[s] to how people understand their relationship to the world, how that relationship is constructed across time and space, and how people understand their possibilities for the future" (1997, 410). Most young people would probably tackle the issue of identity by asking, "Who am I? How do I fit into the world? What is my position at home, in school, in my community? What do I believe? Where have I come from and where am I going?" Native-born youth at some time or another usually ask themselves these questions. For some youth, the process of finding out "Who am I?" can be most difficult. What if they were to add all the problems that come along with being an outsider by virtue of being a non-English-speaking immigrant? Answering those questions would be difficult because of the reception many non-English-speaking persons receive when they enter the country.

de Crevecoeur took for granted the idea of assimilation and peoples' willingness to change allegiances and identities. He also saw the importance of "being received in the broad lap of our great Alma Mater." In other words, the new immigrants' changing allegiances and identities called for those who were already here in America to welcome them into the new country, while at the same time the new immigrants were expected to make changes to "fit in" and learn how to become "American." This change in identity, though, has been difficult, at times almost seemingly impossible, when the new immigrants have felt unwelcome. Their own personal reasons for coming here, how they arrived here, and how they were welcomed has had a direct impact on how well immigrants have integrated into "American" society (Ogbu, 1990).

Although on a much grander scale, the Statue of Liberty and all it represents to newcomers is the equivalent of a homeowner's welcome mat. Unfortunately, "welcome" has too often come to be viewed as part of a mat's or a sign's decoration, not necessarily a true reflection of whether all visitors are truly welcomed. Like unsuspecting visitors to someone's home, many immigrants have come to America assuming they were welcome, only to find out the welcome mat was not meant for them. They have found out the welcome mat cannot always be taken at face value.

How visitors are welcomed and then treated when they enter a home informs them as to how to act and speak. It even plays a large role in deciding the length of the visit and whether the visitor decides to leave and never come back. The situation is no different with new immigrants. Being an immigrant has always been fraught with difficulties, but being a non-English-speaking immigrant (and maybe being an immigrant of color) is even more difficult. Add to that the problems that usually come with being an adolescent in America, and it is quite obvious that young, adolescent, non-English-speaking immigrants often have a none-too-easy task in their quest to maintain or forge new identities and mature into productive citizens.

Some individuals wonder why more recent immigrants do not acculturate or assimilate and become "American" like earlier immigrants. They should keep in mind the reception those immigrants received. For instance, most early colonial immigrants were welcomed into this country and assimilated easily. George Washington expressed the nation's sentiment when he declared "that the 'bosom of America [sic] is open to receive not only the opulent and respectable stranger, but the oppressed and persecuted of all nations and religions, whom we shall welcome to a participation of all our rights and privileges" (Stewart, 1993, 3). Who exactly was Washington inviting? Washington was extending this welcome to northern and western Europeans, such as the English, Germans, and Dutch. These Europeans mostly spoke English and were Protestants. In fact, between 1820 and 1860, 95 percent of all immigrants were from this part of Europe (3). Although the United States has never been homogenous, it was much closer to being so in regard to new immigrants during the colonial period.

Years later, many Americans, former immigrants themselves, did not consider Washington's invitation and welcome to extend to the new wave of immigrants that started arriving during the late 1880s and early 1900s. The majority of immigrants who came to this country during that time came not from northern or western Europe, but from southern and eastern Europe, from such places as Italy, Austria-Hungary, Russia, and the Balkans; many were

Catholic, Eastern Orthodox, or Jewish (Stewart, 1993). Like welcome mats that do not always reflect a homeowner's sentiment, America's largest and most famous welcome mat, the Statue of Liberty and its inscription, was not reflective of the kind of welcome received by many of these new immigrants.

Because of the great influx from southern and eastern Europe, many Americans felt compelled to Americanize this new wave of immigrants who were so culturally different from previous immigrants (Carnevale, 2000). Great efforts were expended toward teaching them English and American ways of thinking and living. In essence, the government, especially through schools, embarked on a campaign to change their identities and allegiances and to act "American." Acting American included learning English. No efforts were made, though, to help them keep their home language. In fact, efforts were made to discourage the use and learning of German and other modern languages, as evidenced in Myer v. Nebraska, a Supreme Court case that overthrew Nebraska's law forbidding the teaching of modern foreign languages.

Although very different peoples began arriving onto American shores during the turn of the century from the 1800s to the 1900s, the greatest change in the face of immigration began after passage of the Immigration and Nationality Act of 1965. Since that year, the greatest number of immigrants to this country have come from Latin America and Asia: "From 1965 to 1995, the United States accepted an estimated forty million immigrants, mostly from third world countries" (Kearny & Heineman, 2002, 196). These new immigrants have been mostly Catholic or non-Christian, non-white, non-English-speaking, with customs, values, and beliefs vastly different from that of mainstream Anglo Americans. For them, changing or redefining their identities is a much more difficult task.

Like the immigrants from several decades before, these new immigrants have not received the same kind of welcome as did the colonial immigrants. The early, or colonial immigrants, had much more in common with their new countrymen than do modern immigrants. The new immigrants, besides being mostly people of color, have very different values and beliefs. For instance, many of them come from collectivist, not individualistic, cultures and some are non-Christian.

For this author, growing up as a Puerto Rican of mixed racial heritage in New Jersey, the issue of identity was always paramount. As a light-skinned Puerto Rican with kinky hair and green eyes, I many times aroused curiosity. I often heard the question, "What are you?" Whenever I replied, I usually heard one of two comments: "You don't look Puerto Rican" or "You don't sound Puerto Rican." I heard those comments even from fellow Puerto Ricans who could not quite immediately peg me or easily identify my racial and national background. Even when very young, I knew what they meant—I did not look or speak like the stereotypical Puerto Rican. This type of curiosity always confounded me.

I still remember the first day of high school when I entered the cafeteria. White students occupied the left side of the room and black students occupied the right side. I had black, white, and Hispanic friends, and finding a place to sit was not just a matter of finding an empty seat. I knew that where I sat would define me for the rest of the school year. If I sat with my white friends, my black friends would think I was trying to "act white." If I sat with my black friends, my Puerto Rico friends would think I was betraying them. To this day, it still amazes me how much importance I put upon finding a place to sit. I am sure none of my teachers would have understood the inner turmoil I experienced that day. Fortunately for me, after standing at the doorway for what seemed an eternity, I finally spotted one table occupied by some Hispanic students. Hispanics sat on one side of the table and some black students sat on the other side. Serendipitously, I found a seat right in the middle, with Hispanic students to my left and black students to my right. Somehow, in my mind, I knew I had found the right spot for me. The black students to my right helped me reaffirm my blackness and the Hispanic students to my left helped me to reaffirm my national and cultural background. I often found myself speaking English to my friends to the right of me and either Spanish or code switching with Spanish and English with my friends to the left.

I cannot remember a time while growing up that language, race, nationality, beliefs, and values were not an issue for me. My Spanish teacher thought I was taking her class because I wanted an easy A, not because I wanted to learn more about my home language so I could write to my non-English-speaking relatives. Her dislike for Hispanic students was palpable. My guidance counselors were surprised to have a Puerto Rican, a nonnative English speaker, wanting to take honors English classes. Although I was a member of the National Honor Society, I was never given an opportunity to enroll in an honors class. Except for one African American whose parents challenged the school's placement system, I knew of no students of color who were in honors classes. I earned straight As for years in English in high school, yet college admissions demanded I take the Test of English as a Foreign Language (TOEFL) exam to prove I could speak and write English. I went to school with students who had, what I considered at the time, unbridled liberty and freedom. Reconciling myself to behaving like the submissive, never-leaving-the-house-unless-chaperoned good Puerto Rican girl was extremely trying for me. I tried as best I could to explain to my friends why I could not date. I tried to explain how my family was not crazy for eating boiled green bananas. As much as I tried, in many respects, I was always an outsider, someone whose parents did not speak English, someone who ate strange foods, someone who was not considered black or white, and someone who was always trying to dispel the negative stereotypes bestowed upon Puerto Ricans in our community.

Like most immigrant children, cognitively I knew who I was. I knew which little boxes to darken when filling out forms. I knew my language, national, and racial background, but emotionally, I was torn between cultures. As mentioned above, Norton defines identity as "how people understand their relationship to the world, how that relationship is constructed across time and space, and how people understand their possibilities for the future." I did not understand my possibilities for the future. Although a good student, I was not expected to do well in honors classes and so I was not allowed to be in one. Whenever a Spanish-speaking person in the community did something illegal or not to the liking of the school or community, a Puerto Rican was blamed. In a way, I understood my relationship to people in the world, but that relationship was mostly a negative one. As to possibilities for the future, that idea was murky at best; while growing up I knew no middle-class Hispanics or professionals, not even a teacher. The only characters from pop culture I can remember from the time were the Puerto Ricans from *West Side Story.*

To me, the welcome the Statue of Liberty represented was rather hollow. I could see the big picture, and how I was living in and was a part of America, but deep inside, I knew I was not welcome. Although I knew I was not going to be thrown out, deported, I could see I was not treated the same as my white counterparts. I did not live in the better neighborhoods, I was not expected to excel, and so I was not put in classes that fully challenged me. I knew my honest father had stopped shopping at certain stores because as an Afro Puerto Rican he was always followed by security—as if he were going to steal their merchandise. I heard the comments made by classmates about "knife-carrying dirty Puerto Ricans."

Since 1917, Puerto Ricans have been American citizens, so technically, I was not an immigrant, but for all intents and purposes, in my neighborhood I was treated like a nonnative, English-speaking immigrant, an outsider with a different language and customs. What does it mean to be an immigrant? Specifically, what does it mean to be an English-language learner? The two are not the same, although in many people's minds they are. Some immigrants come to America already speaking English as their native language or as a second language. Many though, like myself, come to America not knowing how to speak English or knowing how to productively and easily function in a culture that is vastly different from their own. Their problems are not just language related.

English-language learners have a difficult time because there are so many issues involved in becoming acculturated to American ways: language, "race, class, gender, sexuality, religious affiliation, ability or disability" (Ullman, 1997, 1). All of these issues, along with the kind of welcome extended, play a role in shaping their identity.

Learning English is not just a matter of acquiring new vocabulary and learning when to use it. Similar to learning a first language, learning a second one does not happen in a vacuum. How others perceive English-language learners and how they react to them can do much to either encourage or discourage them in their quest toward learning English and becoming American. Their reception plays an important role in how English-language learners perceive themselves and how they form an identity.

Family Language and Its Importance

"Why don't these people learn English before they come here?" "They don't want to learn English." These and other negative comments are often uttered by individuals who know little about the physical and emotional journey many English-language learners travel before coming to America. Language is not just a matter of syntax, phonemes, and morphemes to be learned in a matter of a few months. It is through language that culture is transmitted. It should not be discarded when a new one becomes more popular or is more in demand. Most teachers of a foreign language would never think of teaching French, Spanish, or any other language without also teaching culture. Why? Both are intertwined. Language is an integral part of culture and reflects the values and beliefs of any particular culture.

According to Ngugi wa Thiong'o, a Kenyan writer who for years has addressed the issue of colonialism and repression in Africa, people see the world and come to an understanding of themselves via language. Language and culture cannot be separated because "language carries culture, and culture carries, particularly through culture and literature, the entire body of values by which we perceive ourselves and our place in the world" (1986, 16).

Many immigrants see their identity closely tied to their language, as demonstrated by a Khmer father:

> I want my daughters to know our culture and our race, as Cambodian people, to be able to identify themselves as Khmer. If my daughters grow up and someone asks them, "What nationality are you?" sometimes I am afraid they will say, "I don't know if I am American or Cambodian or *cham* (Khmer Muslim)!" So they need to know their language and identity. (Smith-Hefner, 1999, 138)

At a time when so many parents are working hard to instill values in their children, teachers, and community leaders should be encouraging children to not forget their family language. Making them forget the family language and encouraging them to speak only English will not help them become more American. If young people are not able to communicate with their parents, they will have a very difficult time answering, "Who am I? How do I fit into the world? What is my position at home, in school, in my community? What do I believe? Where have I come from and where am I going?" A sense of uprootedness and distance from those who love, admonish, and discipline them will not help them at home, school, or the community.

Vietnamese parents in Portland, probably with much sorrow, recognized the importance of family members being able to communicate through a common language:

> If they had only guessed how far their children would drift away from them, separated by the lack of a common language in which to transmit values and family history, they would have never chosen to come to the United States. "We did not want to lose our children to the State in a communist regime, and yet we have totally lost them in a declared democracy." (Ada, 1998, 181)

Unfortunately, not everyone sees or understands the importance of a family language or bilingualism: a Texas judge prohibited a mother from speaking the mother or home language to her child because he deemed it a form of child abuse (Ada, 1998). In order to be good parents, parents must have a common language with their children, one that will work as a conduit to pass on knowledge and wisdom, a common language that will allow parents and children to express respect, love, and family solidarity. Sharing the same knowledge base, culture, and language will help non-English-speaking immigrants with what Portes and Rumbaut refer to as generational dissonance, "when children neither correspond to levels of parental acculturation nor conform to parental guidance, leading to role reversal and parent-child conflicts" (Zhou, 2001, 207).

Racism, Language, and Identity

Weisman notes that "given the fact that the native language is the vehicle through which individuals encode their cultural reality, language becomes intimately connected to a sense of cultural identity" (Weisman, 2001, 208). Unfortunately, it is this very same cultural identity that some individuals feel newcomers should forsake and replace with an American one, for, how else can they expect to succeed? Such individuals should remember that even if they learn English, many immigrants, because of their social class, religion, and especially color, will not be accepted into American society as equal members. After seeing and feeling the injustice of bigotry and racism, some of them come to feel, "Why should I give up my culture, where I am fully welcome, and take on a new one that will never fully accept me, one that will all too often shoo me away off the welcome mat?"

Although many people would like to think racism is in America's past, many new immigrants see racism in this country as an almost insurmountable challenge, a kind of racism that is pervasive, even in the language itself (Moore, 1998). They come to understand that no matter how hard they try to be American, no matter how well they learn to speak English, and no matter how many degrees they earn, they will never enjoy the same privileges usually enjoyed by white Americans (Jensen, 1998). Some of them feel like the Mexican woman who said, "The gringos will always consider us inferior" (Portes & Rumbaut, 1996, 2). No matter how often people individually deny racism, America is still deeply divided by the issues of race.

For years, in this country, "race" meant mainly Black and white. Labeling immigrants either Black or white is no longer feasible, as reflected in America's census, with multiple ways of self-identification (U.S. Census Bureau, 2000). Today's television, movies, magazines, and billboards are often populated with individuals from diverse backgrounds and institutionalized racism and Jim Crow laws as they existed years ago no longer exist, but that does not mean racism does not exist.

Some English-language learners come to America and are bewildered by its definition of race and the stereotypes attached to those who are nonwhite. Many come to this country to face discrimination unlike any they have ever faced in their home countries. They come to a country that defines them first by color, not by their profession, social status, family ties, or the "content of their character" (Carson and Shepard, 2001, 85).

Family

Far too often, individuals do not understand the struggles young English-language learners undergo within their own families as they become conversant in English and learn American culture. Many children are forced to live in two worlds or cultures—the American culture as reflected in school and when they are among their American friends and the culture of the old country as reflected in the home and when they are among family friends (Burgos-Aponte, 2004). Often, these two cultures clash, with the young wanting to assert their independence and be more like their American counterparts (Stepick, Stepick, Eugene, Teed, & Labissiere, 2001).

Although individualism is greatly encouraged in this country, it is often discouraged in non-American cultures. Young people are expected to live by certain rules, rules that may be contradictory to what they see in American schools. For example, Khmer American girls are "expected to . . . keep their eyes downcast and avoid direct eye contact, particularly in the presence of males. It is considered especially important that a girl be shy and demure" (Smith-Hefner, 1999, 99). Young girls are not given the freedom of American girls; when they are not at home, "they are expected to have a companion—a sibling, cousin, or girlfriend—at all times" (Smith-Hefner, 100). Such close supervision can bring about great pressure. Young girls are expected to listen to and obey their parents, but they may also want to enjoy the freedom they see their American peers enjoying.

Such close supervision is not only found among Khmer Americans; it is also found among many Hispanics and Asians. Issues of dating, talking to boys, "dressing out" for physical education classes, and participating in extracurricular activities are not as simple as they are for American girls. Even more difficult for some young immigrants is the role parents from some cultures play in the choosing of a marriage mate for them.

When the children in the household learn English and the parents' English is limited or nonexistent, power struggles may ensue. Because they often play the role of translators, children become privy to information most parents would prefer to keep to themselves. Children sometimes have to serve as translators in schools, courts, hospitals, social service and unemployment offices, and banks. Being privy to the knowledge culled from serving as translators in such situations may give children greater knowledge and authority than most parents would like for their children to have. Some parents find themselves having to rely on their children far too often. Valenzuela (1999) goes to the point of even calling children "surrogate parents" (720). What a reversal of roles! Even more important, though, is the burden and sense of responsibility placed on such children.

Suggestions for Teachers

All teachers know that being proficient in English is one of the keys to success in this country. Knowing how to speak English, though, should not preclude learning and using the family language. In order for parents to be able to communicate with their children, both the parents and the children must have one common language, one that allows for more than just the basic communication that goes on with individuals who happen to live in the same house. Parents must be able to share stories, values, beliefs, fears, and hopes with their children. When they discipline and admonish, they should be able to do so via a common language so that their children can understand the why of the discipline and admonishment.

If at all possible, teachers should encourage the learning and use of both English and the family language, even if bilingual education is not available in their school districts. Too often teachers take the deficit view and concentrate only on the fact that English-language learners do not speak English. "A more positive approach views these students as having bilingual and bicultural skills, skills that will enable them to become productive members in a diverse American culture and in an "expanding global economy" (Rolón, 2003, 41).

Children should not be made to feel embarrassed about their family language. If anything, they should be made to feel proud; how many other students or even teachers are learning to be completely bilingual? Unlike many students in Europe who begin learning a second language in elementary school, most American students do not start to learn a second language until they reach high school. Most teachers would probably agree with former secretary of education Richard W. Riley when he stated, "I see no reason why our children should not be their equals" (1998, 4). In other words, if European children can learn a second and sometimes even a third or fourth language while young, our American students should be able to do the same.

Thiong'o writes that "language as culture is . . . an image-forming agent in the mind of a child. Our whole conception of ourselves as a people, individually and collectively, is based on those pictures" (1986, 15). Often English-language learners have to face an American culture and language that seems to be intent on labeling them with negative stereotypes. The least we as teachers should do is help them keep their family language, one that helps them maintain a positive cultural image.

In this country, extracurricular activities are considered an important part of schooling. Teachers should keep in mind this is not the case in many other parts of the world. Some parents do not want their children to participate in extracurricular activities, especially if boys and girls may interact together. For instance, some parents will not give permission for a daughter to go to school dances or even the prom unless chaperoned. Teachers should encourage, but not continually insist upon, participation in such activities if it is going to cause undue duress to the young person. They should respect the fact that other cultures do not approve of dating and certain extracurricular activities.

In order to understand the social and linguistic challenges students face, school personnel should be trained on issues of diversity and culture. If no training is available, they should read on their own and make an effort to confront their own prejudices and stereotypes. Acknowledging these is important—we all have them. An easy way to begin learning about cultures is to read accounts written by individuals who have had to live simultaneously in more than one culture. In recent years, several easily accessible books have been published. They show the social, racial, and religious struggles individuals face when they are members of cultures that are vastly different from that of the dominant culture (Dumas, 2004; Walker, 2001, Moreno & Mulligan, 2004). Taking time to learn more about students' cultures is a sign that school personnel are willing to recognize students' differences and the challenges they face.

School personnel should not just read about other cultures. Many communities now have sports leagues, businesses, churches, and other places where individuals from other cultures congregate. They should reach out to people in their community because reading can never take the place of actually meeting and talking to people from other cultures.

Teachers should keep in mind the racism some of their students face and the negative impact it can have on how they feel about themselves and their place in this world. This racism is not necessarily the burn-a-cross-in-the-backyard type of racism. Today's racism is often much more subtle and may present itself in deferent guises, such as social shunning, name calling, and even low expectations from teachers and administrators. This type of racism is more like water torture—sometimes not even noticeable and oftentimes its impact denied. Although it is denied, its impact can be negatively life altering.

At a time when we should no longer classify people as just either Black or white, we should also keep in mind that we should allow our students to identify themselves whatever way they choose. Hispanics are not a monolithic group. They have to come to America to be labeled Hispanics. Many prefer to be identified by their country of origin, not by the term "Hispanic" (Acuna, 2000). As Gracia (2000) points out, "There are no properties common to all Hispanics at all times and in all places that are discernible" (56). Most Puerto Ricans and Mexicans may share the same language, but their national histories and struggles have not been the same. Reddick comments how "a shared complexion does not guarantee racial solidarity" (1998, 1).

African Americans and Africans may be viewed the same by many white Americans, but they have very different customs, values, and beliefs. The experience of Vietnamese refugees is very different from Japanese immigrants, and yet they are often grouped together and labeled "Asian." Instead of labeling students as Black, African, Hispanic, or Asian, teachers should allow students to identify themselves and thus show respect for their national culture and identities.

Teachers should also be cognizant of the ill effects of always being questioned about one's racial background. Carmen Wong, a Hispanic with a Chinese surname, writes about how she and other family members

> would be questioned about our racial origins—virtually every day. Everywhere we went. Were we black? "Oreos?" Were we adopted? . . . Chimps in a zoo. Freaks in a freak show . . . the constant you-don't-look Chinese were infecting me under the skin, like mites laying eggs one by one, itching and waiting to hatch. (2004, 211)

Being asked to "justify" or explain one's racial background can be extremely irritating and wearing and often makes individuals unnecessarily question their own background and identity.

Conclusion

Answering the questions, "Who am I? How do I fit into the world? What is my position at home, in school, in my community? What do I believe? Where have I come from and where am I going?" is often very difficult for English-language learners. When they try to answer, "Who am I?" they often find themselves struggling to fit into two cultures that have conflicting beliefs and value systems. Their cultural beliefs are often challenged. Instead of forging an identity for themselves, they sometimes let the outside world form one for them—often to their detriment. These labels and identities that they are expected to conform to are oftentimes based on negative linguistic, national, and racial stereotypes.

As teachers we should help English-language learners balance their two cultures and thus their identities. We should encourage them to speak to their parents in whatever language is common to both parents and children. If they are forgetting their family language, we should encourage them to not do so. This may call for us to be their advocates and encourage them to enter bilingual education programs where the goal is for them to become truly bilingual, fully competent in both languages. If bilingual programs are not available, they should do everything they can either as English to Speakers of Other Languages (ESOL) or regular mainstream teachers to include aspects of the students' culture and language in their classes. Teachers have to help students forge their own identities and not let others with negative stereotypes form it for them. Students should understand that it is possible to acculturate, to learn to take the best of both cultures and form a new identity. They do not have to assimilate and forget their home culture and language. They also do not have to live on the margins of both cultures, not knowing which language and culture with which to identify.

With our help, maybe our students will not feel like Lorenzo Munoz (2004), a Mexican American reporter for the *Los Angeles Times* who had the following to say:

> Perhaps I am bound to never find my place. I wonder if the perfect place is only my mind. The day I learn to love one country unconditionally—just as I do my family—is the day I will know I have matured. When I reach that point, I will be at peace. Until then I will spend my days searching for something that is perhaps unattainable. (166)

Instead, maybe our students can someday feel like Lazarus's words of welcome on the Statue of Liberty can extend to them also. Maybe they will grow up and be able to proudly give answers to the questions of, "Who am I? How do I fit into the world? What is my position at home, in school, in my community? What do I believe? Where have I come from and where am I going?" Answers to these questions do not always come easily, but we as teachers can play a role in helping students answer such questions in a positive manner.

References

Acuna, R. (2000). *Occupied America: A history of Chicanos.* New York: Addison Wesley Longman.

Ada, A. F. (1998). Linguistic human rights and education. In E. Lee, D. Menkart, and M. Okazawa-Rey (Eds.), *Beyond heroes and holidays* (181–84). Washington, DC: Network of Educators on the Americas.

Burgos-Aponte, G. D. (2004). Ethnic identity and self-esteem among high school students. Retrieved October 20, 2006, from fred.ocsu.edu:8000/archive /00000130/02etd-2004-26.html

Carnevale, N. C. (2000). Language, race, and the new immigrants: The example of southern Italians. In N. Foner, R. G. Rumbaut, & S. J. Gold (Eds.), *Immigration research for a new century.* (409–22). New York: Russell Sage Foundation.

Carson C., & Shepard, K. (Eds.) (2001). A call to conscience: The landmark speeches of Dr. Martin Luther King, Jr. New York: Warner Books.

de Crevecoeur, J. H. (1997). *Letters from an American farmer* (S. Manning, Ed.). New York: Oxford University Press.

Dumas, F. (2004). *Funny in Farsi.* New York: Random House.

Gracia, J. J. E. (2000). *Hispanic/Latino identity: A philosophical perspective.* Malden, MA: Blackwell Publishers Ltd.

Jensen, R. (1998, July 19). White privilege shapes the U.S. *Baltimore Sun,* C-1.

Kearny, E. N., & Heineman, R. A. (2002). The silent revolution: Political, ideological and group dimensions of the immigration crisis. *Perspectives on Political Science, 31*(4), 196–203.

Meyer v. Nebraska. (1923). 262 U.S. 390.

Moore, R. B. (1998). Racism in the English language. In E. Lee, D. Menkart, & M. Okazawa-Rey (Eds.), *Beyond Heroes and Holidays: A practical guide to k-12 antiracist, multicultural education and staff development* (166–69). Washington, DC: Network of Educators on the Americas.

Moreno, R., & Mulligan, M. H. (2004). *Border-line personalities.* New York: HarperCollins Publishers.

Munoz, L. (2004). American Girl. In R. Moreno & M. H. Mulligan (Eds.). *Border-line personalities* (155–66). New York: HarperCollins Publisher.

Norton, B. (1997). Language, identity, and the ownership of English. *TESOL Quarterly, 31*(3), 409–29.

Ogbu, J. (1990). Minority education in comparative perspective. *Journal of Negro Education, 59*(1), 45–47.

Portes, A., & Rumbaut, R. G. (1996). *Immigrant America: A portrait.* Berkeley: University of California Press.

Reddick, T. (1998). *African vs. African-American: A shared complexion does not guarantee racial [sic] solidarity.* Retrieved October 25, 2004, from www.library.yale .ed/~fboateng/akata.htm

Riley, R. W. (1998). *Statement by U.S. Secretary of Education Richard W. Riley on California Proposition 227.* Retrieved October 1, 2004, from www.ed.gov/ PressReleases/04-1998/unzst.html

Rolón, C. A. (2003). Educating Latino Students. *Educational Leadership, 60,* 40–43.

Smith-Hefner, N. J. (1999). *Khmer American: Identity and moral education in a diasporic community.* Berkeley: University of California Press.

Stepick, A., Stepick, C. D., Eugene, E., Teed, D., & Labissiere, Y. (2001). Shifting identities and intergenerational conflict: Growing up Haitian in Miami. In R. G. Rumbaut & A. Portes (Eds.), *Ethnicities: Children of immigrants in America* (229–66). Berkeley: University of California Press.

Stewart, D. W. (1993). *Immigration and education: The crisis and the opportunities.* New York: Lexington Books.

Thiong'o, N. W. (1986). *Decolonising the mind: The politics of language in African Literature.* Portsmouth, NH: Heinemann.

Ullman, C. (1997). *Social identity and the adult ESL classroom.* Washington, DC: National Center for ESL Literacy Education.

U.S. Census Bureau. (n.d.). *United States census 2000.* Retrieved November 15, 2004, from www.census.gov/dmd/www/2000quest.html

Valenzuela, A. (1999). Gender roles and settlement activities among children and their immigrant families. *American Behavioral Scientist, 42*(4), 720–42.

Walker, R. (2001). *Black, White, and Jewish.* New York: Putnam.

Weisman, E. M. (2001). Bicultural identify and language attitudes. *Urban Education, 36*(2), 203–25.

Wong, C. R. (2004). Getting it straight. In R. Moreno & M. H. Mulligan (Eds.). *Border-line personalities* (205–23). New York: HarperCollins Publisher.

Zhou, M. (2001). Straddling different worlds: The acculturation of Vietnamese refugee children. In R. G. Rumbaut & A. Portes (Eds.), *Ethnicities: Children of Immigrants in America* (187–227). Berkeley: University of California Press.

5

Identity Formation and Recognition in Asian American Students

Kimberley A. Woo

Mirror, Mirror on the wall. Who (am I among) them all?

Introduction

This paraphrase from a well-known childhood fairy tale speaks to identity formation, a dynamic process in which individuals recast their identities according to the social context in which they find themselves. Identity formation entails individuals measuring their own self-perceptions against others' perceptions of themselves to formulate an identity at a particular place and time.

Historically in the United States, race[1] has been used to categorize persons who are part of larger populations. Reliance on phenotypic traits (e.g., skin color, hair type, and nose shape) as a grouping strategy has had a long tradition in this country and can be useful when analyzing data for political purposes, determining demographic trends, and allocating resources. At the same time, this approach can be detrimental, for it only considers individuals in generalized terms such as racial- or gender-group membership.

85

By contrast, individuals may highlight their ethnicity when asked to self-identify. For example, they might mention such characteristics as national origin, language, religion, and/or food when describing themselves. Because some consider using ethnicity as a means of identification too limited in scope, ethnic experience, though a crucial part of the analytical context, is often overlooked. If ethnicity is acknowledged as an integral aspect of a person's self-identity, the resulting insights increase in usefulness because they can be used to explain the range of experiences between and within ethnic groups.

With these theoretical concerns in mind, this chapter addresses the following in two questions:

1. How have experiences with public education shaped one Asian American[2] student's identity?
2. What are some strategies one Asian American student used to negotiate her identity within the educational context?

A synthesis of literature will contextualize the discussion of Asian American identity formation and of schools. Next, one student's experiences will be analyzed in terms of the impact of others' perceptions and her self-perception in shaping her identity as an Asian American. This chapter ends with an invitation to all stakeholders[3] to think about how they can best support Asian American students in their quest to answer, "Who am I?"

Ambivalent Response to Asians in the United States

The response to the presence of Asian people in the United States has been somewhat schizophrenic, as reflected by the ambivalent treatment they have received in this country, in particular as participants in its education system. Generally speaking, Asians' reception has been contingent upon the overall state of the American economy. During times of economic boom, Asians are often described as "hard workers," "good students," and cultural ambassadors whose presence adds much richness to the cultural fabric of this nation. During less prosperous times, however, these same persons have often been characterized as lazy, sneaky, clannish, economic threats, and even enemies of the United States.

Selected Literature

This ambivalent response to the Asian presence has manifested within the educational arena. Before going further, it must be pointed out that relatively scant information is available regarding Asian American students' experiences, despite the fact that they are the fastest-growing racial or ethnic group in the United States (Nakanishi & Nishida, 1995; Shinagawa & Jang, 1998).

Lee (1996) notes and challenges the claim that Asian American populations are not statistically significant enough to warrant inclusion in large-scale studies. While this exclusion may be valid when examining overall national trends, Lee maintains that this point is not applicable when research focuses on participants from states like California, Hawaii, and New York, which contain some of the largest Asian American populations in the United States. She questions the logic of not separating out Asian Americans as a specific category for analysis, and concludes that, when not seen as a separate entity, their experiences are often subsumed within those of European American majority.

At the same time, Lee points out that Asians have historically been seen as "unassimilable minorities" (1996, 4) and are often described as immigrants. This can erroneously result in perceptions that all Asians are newcomers to this country. Takaki (1989) argues that despite the fact that Asians have lived in the United States for more than 150 years, they will always been seen as "strangers from a different shore."

Lee claims that the exclusion of Asian Americans from the discussion on race results in the silencing of their needs. She argues that most Americans perceive African Americans and Latinos as minorities because they experienced disproportionately high levels of poverty and educational underachievement. As a result, African Americans and Latinos receive a statistically larger percentage of resources, both financial and human, as well as attention in academia.

By contrast, Weinburg (1997) argues, "In the world of educational research and writing, Asian American students occupy little more than the margins . . . Discussions of current educational problems slight their importance when they deign to take notice of them at all" (1). Pang and Cheng (1998) add that "to many teachers, Asian Pacific American children are invisible; though teachers may notice physical differences, their needs are often overlooked" (3).

What little research exists has focused on Asian Americans as members of the "model minority." The origins of this phrase date back to the 1960s. In perhaps a response to blacks' contention that racial injustice was pervasive in the United States, the media presented an image of Asian Americans as a successful minority: "Despite past discrimination, [Asians have] succeeded in becoming a hardworking, uncomplaining minority deserving to serve as a model for other minorities" (Chun, 1980, as cited in Nakanishi & Nishida, 1995, 96). Given the racial unrest of the era, the common usage of the term at that time can be viewed as a mainstream effort to demonstrate that fulfilling the American dream remained possible for anyone, regardless of race.

In any event, Asian Americans continue to be subsumed under the homogenous label of model minority and are believed to be especially gifted academically, particularly in fields that require technical expertise—for example, engineering, computers, mathematics, and sciences (Pang, 1997). LaFromboise, Coleman, and Gerton's (1993) work suggests that Asian Americans' successes can in part be explained because of their willingness to assimilate or acculturate to new surroundings. These researchers differentiate assimilation and acculturation in the following ways:

> The assimilation approach emphasizes that individuals, their offspring, or their cultural group will eventually become full members of the majority culture and lose identification with their culture of origin. By contrast, the acculturation model implies that the individual, while becoming a competent participant in the majority culture, will always be identified as a member of the minority culture. (397)

Both assimilation and acculturation assume individuals' desires to become part of another culture. Many Asian Americans seemingly manifest such a desire to fit in with the majority culture, prompting them to attempt to succeed in European American, middle-class terms. Certainly, Asian Americans often actually experience "success"; statistics show that, nationally, Asian Americans have among the highest household incomes and rates of acceptance into elite colleges. However, while a large number of Asian Americans enjoy success, not all do. Indeed, some Asian ethnic groups such as Hmong, Laotians, and Pacific Islanders experience poverty and school-dropout rates greater than or equal to that of other minority racial and ethnic groups (Pang, 1997; Vang, 1999; Walker-Moffat, 1995). Thus, while assimilationist and acculturationist hypotheses may explain some of the successes experienced by Asian Americans, the theory remains incomplete.

From her work with Sikh immigrants who live in rural California, Gibson (1988) concludes that Asian Americans have developed a third response—accommodation—as one of the strategies they employ to succeed in school and society. Gibson believes that in an effort to conform publicly and avoid or reduce conflict with other Americans, many Punjabis choose in certain situations to defer to the ways of the dominant group when they believe it is in their best interest. Specifically, Gibson argues that Asian Americans consciously make decisions that are most beneficial to their success; they prefer strategies that allow for "mutual adaptation between persons or groups for the purposes of reducing conflict. [This allows] separate group identities and cultures to be maintained" (25). For example, Gibson observed that while many Sikh spoke English in workplace and school settings, when these same persons were at home or elsewhere in their communities, they often spoke Punjab and donned attire that reflected their cultural heritage. Gibson's work demonstrates that while many Sikh publicly recognized the significance of speaking English, they also maintained their culture in their private lives. Gibson maintains that accommodation differs from assimilation or acculturation in that it enables individuals to enjoy success in the majority culture, while retaining intact their identities as members of the minority culture.

As a result of assimilation, acculturation, and accommodation, significant numbers of Asian Americans have experienced success in the United States, success that in part accounts for the model minority myth. Many non-Asians do not understand why the model minority myth might be viewed negatively. They perceive that Asian Americans have embraced this ethos wholeheartedly and indeed enjoy great academic and financial success today. However, this success is hardly universal. What is more, Lee (1996) argues, that the model minority myth overlooks both the struggles and the ultimate achievement of individuals. Worse yet, Lee points out that some Asian Americans internalize the model minority myth as the standard by which they measure their self-worth, thereby establishing expectations that do not allow for different definitions of success and personal satisfaction.

Perhaps most tellingly, Lee contends that, however positively the model minority may be perceived, it does not erase the fact that this myth has been used to pit one minority group against another. She argues that Asian Americans are often cited as a minority group that has overcome discrimination and has achieved more success than even European Americans. "The model minority myth is dangerous because it tells Asian Americans and other minorities how to behave . . . it [the model minority myth] is used against other minority groups to silence claims of inequality" (1996, 125). Lee maintains that this difference in perceptions based on race creates a tension between racial and ethnic groups, because Asian Americans are seen as the "good race," while other minority groups like African Americans and Latinos are seen as "bad race[s]" (5). This dichotomy results in competition and in-fighting among minority groups that might otherwise work together to create a unified front, challenging the inequities that limit minority opportunities.

A Case in Point

Starr[4] was an eighteen-year-old senior at Green High School when we first met. Starr appeared to have it all; she maintained a rigorous course load, received outstanding grades, had many friends, and held a part-time job. She was the seeming embodiment of the model minority myth.

While Starr's life seemed to epitomize success, her experiences also underscored the two-edged sword of being perceived as a member of the model minority. Teachers and school administrators were unanimous in their praise of Starr; they described her as "the perfect student," "a good kid," "hardworking, cooperative," and "earning high marks." In speaking with Starr, however, it became clear that she struggled to maintain the appearance of "the perfect student." Starr admitted that she had decided not to register for the upcoming Advanced Placement (AP) calculus test:

> I didn't study enough in the first semester. I didn't always do my homework. This semester I've been more serious about studying. But I am still afraid I will not score at least a 3, so I am not going to take the exam. As long as I get 90 percent or better grade in the class, my parents will never know that I did not take the AP Calculus test. I am not going to tell them. I don't want them to get mad. I don't want to waste their money. (Woo, 1999)

Starr's decision not to take the AP calculus test was predicated on her feelings of guilt and shame. She felt guilty for not having studied enough during the first semester and feared others' reactions—especially her family's—and her own, if she failed the exam. Rather than risk the outcome, Starr convinced herself that it was better not to waste her parents' money and avoid their anger by not registering for the test at all.

Starr's decision not to take the AP calculus examination supports Sue and Sue's (1972) belief that Asian Americans "fear social stigmatization." Within the context of Asian American social dynamics, many believe that one's behavior reflects that person's upbringing. Thus, when a child does well, her family is often credited for her successes. Similarly, when a child does not do well, blame is placed on her family. Social stigmatization, then, is a strategy that is sometimes used to isolate those persons who are not perceived to be doing well. The hope is that children will strive to do their best in order to avoid shaming their family. In Starr's case, she anticipated not doing well on the AP calculus test and feared that that would result in a "loss of face" in her family's eyes.

Starr's decision not to take this test can also be seen as a response to the stresses she experienced as a result of being perceived as a member of the model minority. "Failure," especially that of a student who had otherwise received the endorsement of her teachers and friends, would result in public humiliation too great for Starr to endure. It is interesting to note that Starr's AP calculus teacher and fellow classmates must have noted her absence during the exam, which may have slightly tarnished her reputation within the Green High School academic community. However, Starr must have felt this was preferable to the mortification of taking the exam and failing it. Starr's fear of academic failure—a failure that would be most painful for someone intent upon meeting the expectations implicit in the model minority myth—precluded her taking academic risks.

Starr's experiences speak to the two-edged sword of being perceived as a member of the model minority. Many believe that Asian Americans, as a group, experience success in all areas of their life. For many Asian American students, this belief has resulted in educators assuming that they are doing well in school. In reality, Asian American students, like other students, experience success in some classes and struggle in others. While both failure and success are natural components of the educational experience, the impact of the model minority stereotype is particularly noteworthy in the lives of many Asian American students who, if they are not actually struggling to succeed academically, are like Starr and coping with pressures imposed upon them by others as well as themselves.

At the same time, Starr sought to disassociate herself from the model minority, insofar as it might result in peer disapproval. She admitted that while many adults idealized Asian American students because they were "hard workers" and "good students," many non-Asian peers demeaned Asian Americans by calling them "herbs"; they were often thought of as "nerds" and "uncool" (e.g., nonathletic, unaware of the latest fashion trends, not interested in popular music and other aspects of mainstream teen culture). While this stereotype did not apply to Starr, she was well aware of it and made sure to dress in a way that she would not be labeled an "herb." During one conversation, Starr revealed that she did not come from a wealthy family. Her father was employed as a chef in a Chinese restaurant six nights a week, and her mother worked part-time as a seamstress to supplement the family's income. Starr admitted that she did not have the means to maintain a trendy wardrobe. Instead, she took a more timeless approach to fashion that was still deemed acceptable by her peers, typically buying her clothes on sale at the Gap. This enabled Starr to avoid being categorized as an "herb" and thus identified with some of the undesirable characteristics attributed to members of the model minority.

While Starr was aware that many of her fellow students possessed a negative opinion of those perceived as members of the model minority, she was also cognizant of a positive role the stereotype played in her life. Starr admitted that, on occasion, she had manipulated others' assumptions about Asian Americans' academic achievement to her advantage. During our first of two interviews, Starr referred to a general perception at Green High School:

> Most Asian people get good grades. If we do something like cut class or walk in the hallway without a pass, we're not going to get in trouble because they [teachers, counselors, and school administration] know we are good students. We get away with a lot of things. (Woo, 1999)

When I asked Starr for an example, she said that she intentionally scheduled our interview during her seventh-period music class, as opposed to a noninstructional time before or after school, study break, or lunchtime. Starr said that it was known throughout Green High that this study had received both Board of Education approval and the support of the Green High School administration. Starr felt that if questioned about missing music class, she could explain that she was involved in "Ms. Woo's research project," and her absence would be categorized as legitimate and not a "cut." In addition, Starr explained that the third-quarter marking period was over and that she was assured that she would receive at least a 90 percent grade. As I was curious about the treatment other students might receive in similar circumstances, I asked Starr, "And what if you were not Asian American? Chinese? How might the teachers and administration respond to an absence?" Starr replied:

> Other kids, like the blacks, Latinos and whites, if they cut class, they'd probably get in trouble. The counselors, they would call

their houses. And the teachers, they would not excuse their absences as easily. (Woo, 1999)

Starr's characterization of the teachers' and the administration's response to non-Asian students' unexcused absences is especially revealing, for she perceives that different "rules" apply to Asian as opposed to non-Asian students at Green High School. While Starr understood that cutting class was not acceptable at Green High School, she was able to rationalize her actions by relying on her strong grades and on others' assumptions about her being a member of a "successful" monolithic racial group. It is almost admirable how clever Starr was in being able to assess the school culture and manipulate the model minority myth to her advantage. Her example might be useful when thinking about how schools and educational stakeholders might respond to the multifaceted needs of Asian American students.

Conclusion and Educational Implications

Before going further, it must be noted that, while snapshots of Starr's life will be used to inform suggestions offered hereafter, this chapter provides a look at just one student's experiences at a specific time and place. Lightfoot (1983) reminds readers to think about how the act of retelling experiences is like that of taking a photograph; both the resulting narrative and image freeze the event in time. With that said, it is now time to revisit the questions posed at the beginning of the chapter.

How Have Experiences With Public Education Shaped One Asian American Student's Identity

Two perspectives clearly influenced Starr's thinking and actions: others' views and her own views of herself as an Asian American student. Starr worked hard to avoid negative judgments; fears of failure and social stigmatization motivated her avoidance of academic and social risks. While it appeared that Starr's 90 percent average would result in an A grade for the class, her forecast of "underachievement" precluded her from taking the end-of-the-year examination that might have added to her prestige and given her college credit and advance standing as an undergraduate—some primary reasons many students enroll in AP courses. By extension, a fear of failure might prevent her from venturing into other risk-taking experiences later in life—for example, not exploring career possibilities outside the purview typically affiliated with Asian American success.

At the same time, Starr made a concerted effort to avoid being identified with the undesirable traits associated with the model minority. Her decisions regarding what she wore to school were influenced by her not wanting to be considered an Asian American "herb."

What are Some Strategies One Asian American Student Used to Negotiate Her Identity Within the Educational Context?

Starr's academic and social astuteness enabled her to maintain the façade of success despite the reality of her inner conflicts. Starr's decisions regarding not taking the AP calculus examination and the scheduling of our first interview revealed a complex understanding about the dynamics of being perceived as "successful" and indeed a willingness to manipulate the success to her advantage.

How Can Educational Stakeholders Best Support Asian American Students in Their Quest to Answer "Who am I?"

Given the breadth and depth of Starr's experiences, persons involved with all aspects of education must wonder how they can best support Asian American students. A few suggestions come quickly to mind.

First, increasing awareness through preservice and in-service training regarding the impact of monolithic labels would nuance teachers' thinking about their students' experiences, particularly those of Asian ancestry. Increased knowledge regarding historical, geopolitical, cultural, religious, and gender particularities of Asian ethnic groups is one way educators can counteract the influence of the model minority myth in their dealings with Asian American students.

Next, it is important to realize that knowledge for knowledge's sake is often not sufficient to initiate change of perspectives. Thus, I would like to suggest that as part of teachers' training, they engage in sustained and meaningful interactions with Asian American individuals. Chatting on list servers, participating in dialogues that explore Asian American community issues, and attending panels or focus groups should reinforce awareness about differences that exist between and within Asian ethnic groups. Seeing students, particularly Asian American students, as complex persons with specific needs (e.g., language development, academic skills, counseling, and access to economic resources) is one way to decrease the likelihood that their concerns will be overlooked.

Finally, perhaps the most important means of supporting Asian American students in their ever-evolving identities is allowing them to speak for themselves. While it is administrators' responsibility to provide environments that offer equal access and delivery of services to all students, too often the allocation of resources takes place void of the would-be beneficiaries' input. For example, Asian American students could be encouraged to review text, provide feedback, and suggest activities and supplements to strengthen curricula. When discussing Asian American history, Asian American students and/or members from their families might be invited to share their own reasons for immigrating to the United States and discuss how moving to another country has impacted their lives. All the while, it is important to remember that while some Asian Americans are recent immigrants to the United States, there are others who have lived here for many generations. Thus, it would be the teacher's responsibility to not make immigration-related assumptions based on students' appearances.

It is hoped that the recommendations provided herein will influence all who are a part of the educational process; the intent of this research is to create and sustain learning environments that celebrate the multiple ways students experience success. More specifically, I hope that this work encourages teachers and students, particularly those students of Asian decent, to look boldly into the magic mirror of their lives, to appreciate their ever-changing reflections, to challenge stereotypical assumptions, and to embrace the many possibilities that can be a part of their futures.

Notes

1. Mittelberg & Waters (1992, as cited by Tuan, 1998, 21) state, "Race has been used by theorists to refer to distinctions drawn from physical appearance. Ethnicity has been used to refer to distinctions based on . . . cultural markers."

2. When writing about people of color, some authors use hyphens, e.g., Asian-American, while others do not, e.g., Asian American. Some authors also use single ethnic descriptors rather than hyphenated or non-hyphenated descriptors, e.g., Asian rather than Asian American or Asian-American. In addition, some authors capitalize the first letter of racial or ethnic descriptors, e.g., black, while others do not. The use or absence of the hyphen, the inclusion or non-inclusion of the qualifier "American," and the decision whether or not to capitalize ethnic descriptors have major political and psychological implications which go beyond the scope of this work. When quoting authors, I use terminology, capitalization, and spellings that are consistent with their work.

3. Many people are a part of the education process—students, teachers, school administrators and counselors, tutors, parents, other students, members of the extended family, community members, policymakers, and so on. The term *stakeholder* will be used to describe all persons who are involved with the education of our children.

4. For this study of which Starr was a part, pseudonyms were used to protect participants' and schools' identities. Students were given the opportunity to select their own names. In this student's case, she told me she wanted to be called *Starr* because she wanted to be the "star" in her parents' life.

References

Chun, K. T. (1995). The myth of Asian American success and its educational ramifications. In D. T. Nakanishi & T. Y. Nishida (Eds.), *The Asian American educational experience: A sourcebook for teachers* (95–115). New York: Routledge.

Gibson, M. A. (1988). *Accommodation without assimilation: Sikh immigrants in an American high school.* Ithaca, NY: Cornell University Press.

LaFromboise, T., Coleman, H. L. K., & Gerton, J. (1993). Psychological impact of biculturalism: Evidence and theory. *Psychological Bulletin, 114*(3), 395–412.

Lee, S. (1996). *Unraveling the "model minority" stereotype: Listening to Asian American youth.* New York: Teachers College.

Lightfoot, S. L. (1983). *The good high school: Portraits of character and culture.* New York: Basic Books.

Nakanishi, D. T., & Nishida, T. Y. (Eds.). (1995). *The Asian American educational experience: A source book for teachers and students*. New York: Routledge.

Pang, V. O. (1997). Caring for the whole child: Asian Pacific American Students. In J. J. Irvine (Ed.), *Critical knowledge for diverse teachers and learners* (149–88). Washington, DC: American Association of Colleges for Teacher Education.

Pang, V. O., & Cheng, L. L. (1998). *Struggling to be heard: The unmet needs of Asian Pacific American children*. Albany: State University of New York.

Shinagawa, L. H., & Jang, M. (1998). *Atlas of American diversity*. Walnut Creek, CA: Alta Mira.

Sue, D. W., & Sue, S. (1972). Counseling Chinese-Americans. *Personnel and Guidance Journal, 50*, 637–44.

Takaki, R. (1989). *Strangers from a different shore*. New York: Penguin Books.

Tuan, M. (1998). *Forever foreigners or honorary whites? The Asian ethnic experience today*. New Brunswick, NJ: Rutgers University.

Vang, A. (1999). Hmong-American students: Challenges and opportunities. In C. C. Park & M. M. Chi (Eds.), *Asian-American education: Prospects and challenges* (218–36). Westport, CT: Bergin & Garvey.

Walker-Moffat, W. (1995). *The other side of the Asian American success story*. San Francisco: Jossey-Bass.

Weinberg, M. (1997). *Asian American education: Historical background and current realities*. Mahwah, NJ: Lawrence Elrbaum Associates.

Woo, K. A. (1999). "Double happiness," double jeopardy: Exploring ways in which ethnicity, gender, and high school influence the social construction of identity in Chinese American girls. Unpublished dissertation. New York: Teachers College.

6

Curriculum and Recognition

Raymond A. Horn Jr.

As indicated by the title of Charles Bingham's (2001) book, a consideration of recognition is directly related to identity politics and classroom practices. Identity politics is a broad term that includes many issues such as student identity, teacher identity, and the identities that others desire to construct within teachers and students. The construction of how one sees oneself and how others see that individual is a political process with grave implications concerning how power is arranged within a school, community, and nation.

The process of identity formation involves a plethora of contexts including historical, political, economic, cultural, social, and personal. For instance, the identity of a student and teacher in Texas, whether white, African American, or Hispanic, reflects the historical events of that region; past and current arrangements of power; the past and current socioeconomic status of each demographic group and their opportunities for advancement; religious beliefs, language, dress, and other aspects of culture; the regional norms, mores, and laws that govern behavior within and among these groups as well as the cultural messages and influences provided by the larger culture through mass media; and their personal background that includes influences from family, friends, and community members as well as their own genetic endowments and physical and mental health. Central to this process of identity formation is the school that provides a site for all of these contexts to intersect.

The primary concern of this chapter is one aspect of the school—curriculum. However, curriculum is not an isolated element of schooling, but is interconnected and interrelated with all of the previously mentioned contexts. There are many different definitions or types of curriculum such as written, taught, and tested curriculum. Different views of curriculum also can be distinguished by their focus, such as curriculum that is focused on implementing content, curriculum that focuses on the experiences of the learners, curriculum that is focused on the systematic organization of content and delivery that is often known as scope and sequence, or curriculum that is focused on a field of study within education.

Another important type of curriculum is known as the hidden curriculum. This definition of curriculum is concerned with all activity that occurs in the school that affects the classroom without the knowledge of the teachers or students and that occurs but is not disclosed in the written, taught, or tested curriculum. The hidden curriculum focuses on the values, beliefs, and opinions attached to the instructional materials, learner, system, theory, or content.

Those who are concerned about the hidden curriculum take a broader view of what constitutes curriculum (Giroux, 1991; Giroux & Purpel, 1983). They believe that messages and values permeate all classrooms and schools from seemingly noneducational sources such as mass media (i.e., television, movies, music, and print media such as books, magazines, and newspapers), computer-mediated sources such as the Internet, government and political activity, business and market interests, lifestyle issues, community concerns and events, the activity of ideological and philosophical interest groups, religious groups, societal issues and events, labor and management relationships, and sexual preference issues.

Individuals from the field of cultural studies believe that the hidden curriculum is a text that is read by children, not only out of school but also within school. They further believe that when children interpret their experiences, their interpretations are mediated and informed by this hidden curriculum. In other words, the values, beliefs, opinions, and actions of children are affected by the values that are attached to the hidden curriculum. Those who hold this view believe that all curriculum is political in that it is an attempt to promote a specific arrangement of power. In his critique of the core curriculum proposed by E. D. Hirsch Jr. (Hirsch, 1988; Hirsch, Kett & Trefil, 1988), Bingham (2001) states, "It is important to note the political territory that such a curriculum keeps certain cultural groups from occupying" (39–40).

Another important aspect of curriculum involves whether it is a technical, rational curriculum that promotes technical standards, or a critical curriculum that is based upon standards of complexity (Horn, 2004). The former view of curriculum is characterized by curriculum constructed by experts external to the school setting. In this view, the role of teachers is to transmit the required curriculum and the attached values to students who passively receive the information. The current standards and accountability reforms that are primarily based on standardized testing are an example of technical rational curriculum.

In contrast, a critical perspective on curriculum poses standards of complexity (Kincheloe, 2001) that involves student participation in the educational process, the development of critical higher-order thinking skills that students use to interrogate knowledge within the context of their lived experience, and the development of habits that are the foundation for life-long learning. In addition, standards of complexity promote a positive integration of emotions and cognition, students actively posing and solving authentic and relevant problems, the incorporation of themes from the students' daily lives in curriculum, and the facilitation of the development of democratic ideals of social justice, caring, and democratic participation (Shor, 1992). This view of curriculum is more commonly seen in the elite private schools.

In his discussion of textual mirroring, Bingham (2001) mentions, "One way that students can be recognized in the public space of school is by looking to written sources for mirroring" (35). In this context, technical standards require the use of externally produced textbooks, computer-mediated materials, and other written resources that present a predetermined view of content. Conversely, standards of complexity systems promote student research of a topic and require students to critique all resources they access and the conclusions they draw. Another source of written curriculum is the standardized test that promotes answers that are deemed as correct by the constructors of the test. Of course, the attached values are then also to be considered the correct values. A critical perspective on assessment utilizes multiple and authentic assessments that require student reflection and critique on what they learned and on how they learned.

What then does curriculum have to do with identity formation and recognition? First, school is a site of identity formation. Some individuals either naively or disingenuously propose that schools are merely locations where students receive the information and skills necessary to participate in the workforce, acquire citizenship skills and attitudes, and become socialized in the cultural capital that will promote their entrance into mainstream society. In actuality, schools are microcosms of our larger society and provide an important structure for the formation of student identity. What students learn about themselves and others while in school establishes a solid foundation for who they are the rest of their lives. The complexity of identity formation is mirrored by the complexity of their school experience.

Second, because of this seminal social experience, the concept of recognition allows us to understand the educational practices, whether visible or hidden, that affect the formation of student identity and how those identities encounter difference in others. As Bingham (2001) notes,

> The school is an important venue for mirroring because of its public nature. The self needs acknowledgment in the public place of school. Unlike the home or other spaces in which one seeks recognition from friends or significant others, one must find oneself anew in the public arena of school. (34)

This chapter will explore the intersection of curriculum, identity formation, and recognition by discussing the complexity of identity formation, the politics of recognition, and the reconceptualization of curriculum.

The Complexity of Identity Formation in Schools

Like the formal and hidden curriculum encountered by students, schools are sites where political, economic, cultural, social, and personal contexts intersect. All of these contexts impact the formation of student identity. At this site, students are immersed in a complex web of interrelated contexts that provide confirmation and conflict as to who they are and who they will be. In any grade level, students bring preestablished understandings about who they are and about their capabilities and potential.

These personal understandings are first mediated by their interaction with the school environment. How they are perceived and received by faculty and administration, peers, friends, and strangers provides input into their evolving sense of self. The organization of the school into grades, tracks, and unofficial educational and peer groupings mediates their ongoing critique of their identity. Other significant influences are the type of curriculum they encounter, instructional techniques, instructional materials, and assessments. As mentioned, technical standards and standards of complexity have the potential to direct the formation of identity in either restrictive or emancipatory ways.

Whether teaching to a test is the primary instructional method or whether teachers employ best practices based on constructivism, learning styles, multiple intelligences, and brain-based learning, all impact student identity. Individualized and cooperative learning strategies affect what each student learns about oneself, difference, and others in different ways. Assessment with a focus on ranking and sorting students, mastery learning, or portfolios that provide a holistic view of the students not only send messages about oneself, but also impact student considerations about their possibility for later learning and their future position in society.

Also complicit in identity formation and a vibrant part of the school environment are the external interests that attempt to achieve their goals within the school setting. Business interests attempt to develop habits of consumption, employment skills, and workplace attitudes in students (Business Roundtable, 1996; Tucker & Codding, 1998). While in the school setting, students are viewed as a captive market that can be tapped within that environment or conditioned to consume products when outside of school. Much has been written about the market strategies within schools by businesses such as Channel One, the food, footwear, clothing, and other industries (Giroux, 1994; Kohn & Shannon, 2002; Saltman, 2000). As underfunded schools succumb to reimbursement for corporate endorsements, students are made vulnerable to the solicitations of corporate America.

To save on worker-training costs, the business sector lobbies government to more aggressively shift the purpose of schooling from the promotion of citizenship and personal development to vocational tracking and training, as evidenced by the appropriation of school curriculum for vocational pathways and school-to-work programs. Businesses provide free training programs and computer hardware to run software programs that align student learning with the interests of business. It is important to note that along with all of these initiatives come the values deemed important by business interests.

Also, political and ideological interests attempt to reproduce their ideas and values within the school. Through lobbying efforts and attempts to politically control school boards and state educational agencies, curriculum and assessment become contested sites between competing noneducational interests. The influence of special interests on textbook publishers mediates what knowledge, attitudes, values, and skills are presented to students (Giordano, 2003). Control of educator and school certification and accreditation guarantees control of teacher, administrator, and school board compliance with the goals of the special interests. When schools fail to meet state or national standards that represent one specific set of values, public schools may lose local control or fall prey to privatization and school choice initiatives (Bracey, 2002; 2003). All of this interest-group activity represents the hidden curriculum that is imposed on students and that affects their identity formation (Steinberg & Kincheloe, 1997).

Bingham (2001) states, "Attention must be paid not only to the one recognized but to the one recognizing as well" (143). This thought can be applied not only to student-student interactions, but also to educator-student interactions. In this complex web of interrelated contexts, the identity of teachers and administrators is also affected by the activity of special interests. As a special interest gains influence in the school setting, educators adapt and their adaptations influence their students. In some instances, changing curriculum and assessment fosters a concomitant change in how they perceive certain students.

If test scores are disaggregated and a negative outcome for the school is attributed to a certain group of students, these students are then viewed differently by teachers, administrators, and the community. This change in perception may lead to changes in how these individuals are handled and, in turn, have significant consequences for them. Old stereotypes may gain a new credence that is deleterious to the identity formation of those students. The identity of educators is also a project under continuous construction and changes in their identity impacts student identity formation, thus increasing the complexity of the school environment that students encounter.

The Politics of Recognition

Recognition within a school setting is significantly influenced by the culture wars that have raged throughout American history. Herbert Kliebard (1995) detailed the various interests that vied for control of American education from the 1800s to the middle of the twentieth century. While many of these interests can be described in economic and political terms, intended cultural dominance is the underlying agent. In other words, which cultural perspective becomes the dominant culture and therefore has the advantage in reproducing its knowledge and values is the important issue in understanding changes that have occurred in American education. The liberal reforms of education in the 1960s and 1970s were indicative of the larger cultural changes that were occurring in American society. In the 1980s with the conservative restoration during the Reagan administration, education was once again and continues to be restructured to promote a conservative view of American culture. In both cases, education became an important battleground because, quite literally, the children of America are America's future.

Culture *wars*? The military metaphor may be a bit melodramatic, but for a decade these so-called wars have indeed agitated the American educational scene, remolding curricula, revising canons, perplexing administrators, infuriating alumni, and otherwise disturbing the peace.

Arthur M. Schlesinger Jr. (1998), in *The Disuniting of America: Reflections on a Multicultural Society*, indicates the intensity of the conflict between two different perspectives on which cultural view should dominate America. "The fundamental difference between the two positions involves whether a common culture, that assimilates groups who differ from the established culture, or whether a multicultural view, that values difference and diversity, becomes the dominant culture" (Horn, 2002, 90). The culture wars rage in all aspects of education including curriculum. As an example, a well-documented battle (Evans, 2004; Nash, Crabtree & Dunn, 2000; Stotsky, 2000; Symcox, 2002) over curriculum occurred in the 1990s when the *National History Standards* (National Center for History in the Schools, 1996) and the *Expectations of Excellence: Curriculum Standards for Social Studies* (National Council for the Social Studies, 1994) were released.

Despite being created over a period of years with input by classroom practitioners and university professors, both sets of standards were assailed by the religious and mainstream Right as containing inappropriate content and skills; specifically, the references to multiculturalism, globalism, and critical thinking were construed as rewriting history (Gaddy, Hall, & Marzano, 1996; Schmidt, 1997).

The experience with history and social studies curriculum is an example of how special interest groups attempt to colonize student identity through the control of curriculum and through the control of teachers who are restricted to a mandated curriculum. In fact, this colonization can be further expedited through the alignment of mandated curriculum with instruction and assessment methods that reinforce the values that are promoted in the curriculum.

In a pluralist society such as the United States, attempts to promote a specific cultural view represent a politics of recognition. In a discussion of Charles Taylor's ideas on mirroring, Bingham (2001) points out, "Multicultural societies need to mirror back, in a positive way, the cultural communities of diverse individuals" (15). In schools where curriculum represents only one cultural view, many students do not recognize that aspect of their selves when they encounter the pervasive unfamiliarity of mandated curriculum. When curriculum that represents a predominately white, male, and Eurocentric view is encountered, students from that background find themselves well mirrored in that curriculum because the cultural assumptions embedded within the curriculum are familiar.

In recognition theory, the idea of subjection recognizes that cultural norms already in existence mediate the process of recognition. When certain cultural norms are selected as appropriate for reproduction through the educational process and others are not, student identity formation is consequently affected. Students of the unrepresented cultures experience a misrecognition that can be manifested as nonrecognition, in that they experience no affirmation, or malrecognition, in that they experience curriculum that is an affront to their dignity or runs counter to their self-image.

In actuality, misrecognition is an acceptable outcome to those of the dominant culture who desire to reproduce only their cultural perspective. In this case, the intersubjective experience is devoid of reciprocity because the curriculum that represents only one cultural perspective refuses to recognize the Other's perspectives. This lack of reciprocity is also a political tactic used in the colonization of student identity.

The Reconceptualization of Curriculum: Enhancing Diverse Student Identities

In the field of curriculum, over the last three decades critical educators have provided a significant counterpoint to technical-rational curriculum (Pinar, Reynolds, Slattery & Taubman, 1995; Aronowitz & Giroux, 1991). How they have reconceived curriculum aligns with the egalitarian and emancipatory intent of recognition theory. A primary goal of curriculum within the critical perspective is to facilitate in students, teachers, and administrators the development of a critical awareness that through critical literacy leads to action that promotes a socially just, caring, and democratic society. Paulo Freire (1985; 1996) characterized this process as praxis, in that individuals, through the development of a critical literacy, would become critically aware and take emancipatory action that is mediated and informed through a continuous process of critical reflection (Brookfield, 1995; Carr & Kemmis, 1986; Kincheloe, 1993).

One aspect of this critical reflection on one's praxis is that all of the cultural assumptions that one encounters within oneself or in others are critically contextualized and interrogated. Informed by poststructural feminist and postmodern thought, all signs, symbols, and behaviors of human culture and society are also critically interrogated through a reconceptualized curriculum. This area of critical critique enhances the curricular mirroring of the cultural and social diversity found in human relationships. More specifically, it fosters a critical understanding of the interpersonal mirroring that is a significant part of the hidden curriculum.

Critical curriculum is also critically pragmatic in that it facilitates the knowledge and skill that is necessary in order to interrogate the consequences of one's actions in relation to issues of social justice, caring, and democratic participation (Cherryholmes, 1988, 1999). A critical pragmatic orientation relies upon individuals' ability to engage in postformal inquiry (Kincheloe, 1998; Kincheloe, Steinberg & Hinchey, 1999). In relation to the politics of recognition and the central role of cultural assumptions in curriculum, postformal inquiry requires individuals to acquire and use a plethora of inquiry methods and knowledge bases to critically explore the assumptions' origins, the broad and deep context in which they occur, and the larger and hidden cultural and social patterns in which they are embedded.

When individuals post-formally inquire, they ask questions such as: Who benefits and loses because of the assumption? What are the related political, economic, social, and personal contexts of the assumption? What are the critical consequences of these assumptions in terms of power arrangements? What are the larger patterns that they are a part of and how are seemingly unrelated phenomena connected? What masks the intent and hidden consequences of the assumption? While answering these questions, students critically explore their subjection to cultural assumptions that represent the hegemonic norms of their culture and society. In this way, reconceptualized curriculum facilitates the development of diverse student identities, and it promotes student resistance to the colonization that occurs through the politics of recognition.

In a sense, the post-formal process is a process that focuses on personal misrecognition in that attempts to control the recognition process are uncovered and through critical awareness students can take personal and social action to offset attempts to control their identity and to find positive acknowledgment.

In a Deweyan sense, students function as researchers in a student-centered curriculum. Through an awareness of curriculum-as-representation (Bingham, 2001, 104), students can reclaim curricular representations as sources of positive recognition. Furthermore, a reconceptualized curriculum in which students give direction to their own learning and critically interrogate their assumptions and what they learn provides the potential for the unknowability that is required in the act of confirmation. As they develop a healthy and critical skepticism, they understand the critical consequences that arise from preconceived notions about others. In their critical skepticism, they empower themselves and others by continuously questioning their assumptions about themselves and others. In this way, they are also empowered as they engage the ongoing process of the formation of their identity.

Conclusion

Identity formation like critical praxis is a work in progress—an ongoing critical project that requires personal growth over time. As Bingham (2001) notes, "A struggle against misrecognition must be fraught with threat as well as aspiration" (49). The process of becoming critically aware requires engagement with considerations of whiteness, religion, sexual preference, and alternative lifestyles, all of which requires a struggle between what one has come to believe, and the socially just and caring beliefs that one desires to emulate.

Reflection on issues such as these goes beyond recognition that simply confirms existence and requires recognition of an aspect of one's identity that is at odds with the dominant cultural beliefs. The challenge is not to further entrench those beliefs in one's identity but to recognize them as further challenges that must be met. The severity of these challenges can be lessened if they are engaged within a curriculum that supports students in their ability to recognize themselves as well as others in a positive and egalitarian manner.

References

Aronowitz, S., & Giroux, H. (1991). *Postmodern education: Politics, culture, and social criticism*. Minneapolis: University of Minnesota Press.

Bingham, C. (2001). *Schools of recognition: Identity politics and classroom practices*. New York: Rowman & Littlefield.

Bracey, G. W. (2002). *The war against America's public schools: Privatizing schools, commercializing education*. Boston: Allyn & Bacon.

Bracey, G. W. (2003). *On the death of childhood and the destruction of public schools*. Portsmouth, NH: Heinemann.

Brookfield, S. D. (1995). *Becoming a critically reflective teacher*. San Francisco: Jossey-Bass.

Business Roundtable. (1996). *A business leader's guide to setting academic standards*. Washington, DC: Author.

Carr, W., & Kemmis, S. (1986). *Becoming critical: Education, knowledge and action research*. Philadelphia: Falmer Press.

Cherryholmes, C. H. (1988). *Power and criticism: Poststructural investigations in education*. New York: Teachers College Press.

Cherryholmes, C. (1999). *Reading pragmatism*. New York: Teachers College Press.

Evans, R. W. (2004). *The social studies wars: What should we teach the children?* New York: Teachers College Press.

Freire, P. (1985). *The politics of education: Culture, power and liberation*. New York: Bergin & Garvey.

Freire, P. (1996). *Pedagogy of the oppressed*. New York: Continuum.

Gaddy, B. B., Hall, T. W., & Marzano, R. J. (1996). *School wars: Resolving our conflicts over religion and values*. San Francisco: Jossey-Bass Publishers.

Girodano, G. (2003). *Twentieth-century textbook wars: A history of advocacy and opposition*. New York: Peter Lang.

Giroux, H. (1991). *Postmodernism, feminism, and cultural politics: Redrawing educational boundaries*. New York: State University of New York Press.

Giroux, H. (1994). *Disturbing pleasures: Learning about popular culture*. New York: Routledge.

Giroux, H. A., & Purpel, D. (Eds.). (1983). *The hidden curriculum and moral education: Deception or discovery?* Berkeley, CA: McCutchan Publishing Co.

Hirsch, E. D., Jr. (1988). *Cultural literacy: What every American needs to know*. New York: Vintage Books.

Hirsch, E. D., Jr., Kett, J. F., & Trefil, J. (1988). *The dictionary of cultural literacy.* Boston: Houghton Mifflin.

Horn, R. A. (2002). *Understanding educational reform: A reference handbook.* Denver, CO: ABC-CLIO.

Horn, R. A., Jr. (2004). *Standards primer.* New York: Peter Lang.

Kincheloe, J. L. (1993). *Toward a critical politics of teacher thinking: Mapping the post-modern.* Westport, CT: Bergin & Garvey.

Kincheloe, J. L. (Ed.). (1998). *The Post-formal thinking defined.* New York: Guilford Press.

Kincheloe, J. L. (2001). See your standards and raise you: Standards of complexity and the new rigor in education. In R. A. Horn & J. L. Kincheloe (Eds.), *American standards: Quality education in a complex world—The Texas case* (347–68). New York: Peter Lang.

Kincheloe, J. L., Steinberg, S. R., & Hinchey, P. (Eds.). (1999). *The Post-formal reader: Cognition and education.* New York: Garland Press.

Kliebard, H. M. (1995). *The struggle for the American curriculum: 1893-1958* (2nd Ed.). New York: Routledge.

Kohn, A., & Shannon, P. (2002). *Education, inc.: Turning learning into a business.* Portsmouth, NH: Heinemann.

Nash, G. B., Crabtree, C., & Dunn, R. E. (2000). *History on trial: Culture wars and the teaching of the past.* New York: Vintage Books.

National Center for History in the Schools. (1996). *National standards for History.* Los Angeles: Author.

National Council for the Social Studies. (1994). *Expectations of excellence: Curriculum standards for social studies.* Washington, DC: National Council for the Social Studies.

Pinar, W., Reynolds, W., Slattery, P., & Taubman, P. (1995). *Understanding curriculum.* New York: Peter Lang.

Saltman, K. J. (2000). *Collateral damage: Corporatizing public schools—A threat to democracy.* New York: Rowman & Littlefield.

Schlesinger, A. M., Jr. (1998). *The disuniting of America: Reflections on a multicultural society.* New York: W. W. Norton & Co.

Schmidt, A. J. (1997). *The menace of multiculturalism: Trojan horse in America.* Westport, CT: Praeger.

Shor, I. (1992). *Empowering education: Critical teaching for social change.* Chicago: University of Chicago Press.

Steinberg, S. R., & Kincheloe, J. L. (Eds.). (1997). *Kinderculture: The corporate construction of childhood.* Boulder, CO: Westview Press.

Stotsky, S. (Ed.). (2000). *What's at stake in the k-12 standards wars: A primer for educational policy makers.* New York: Peter Lang.

Symcox, L. (2002). *Whose history? The struggle for national standards in American classrooms.* New York: Teachers College Press.

Tucker, M. S., & Codding, J. B. (1998). *Standards for our schools: How to set them, measure them, and reach them.* San Francisco: Jossey-Bass.

7

Extracurricular Activities and Student Identity: Participation in Fine Arts Activities

Amanda M. Rudolph

The public education system in America is faced with many challenges in the twenty-first century, including standardized testing, challenging curricula, student achievement, retention, crime, language diversity, and funding, to name but a few. With all the educational issues making headlines today, very few address extracurricular activities and the students who participate in them. There are occasional features about championship-winning teams in the local papers. There are recaps of the county fair winners. There are pictures of the band during competition. But the majority of the discussion of educational reformation is centered on core curriculum and student achievement.

This phenomenon raises some interesting questions. What is the role of extracurricular activities in school? Why are they included? What do the students gain from participation in an extracurricular activity? How does the recognition from these activities affect students' identities? This chapter will attempt to answer these questions and others related to students and extracurricular activities.

A discussion about all extracurricular activities and implications for students would be unwieldy. Therefore, for the scope of this chapter, extracurricular activities will be limited to the arts, which encompass band, choir, drama, dance, visual arts, and combinations of all of those disciplines. Another chapter specifically addresses issues connected to athletics and recognition and students' identity formation.

The purpose of this chapter is twofold. First, the chapter will provide research to support involvement in extracurricular activities as a positive influence on identity formation for students and will then provide a rationale for promoting the arts as a viable extracurricular opportunity for students. Second, the chapter will discuss the benefits of participation in the arts by students, including a positive self-concept and a greater sense of multicultural awareness as well as benefits for the school itself.

Student Identity and Involvement in Extracurricular Activities

To begin an investigation into the benefits of extracurricular activities, specifically the arts on student identity, it is imperative to construct a sound basis for the argument. The question is: Is participation in any extracurricular activity beneficial for students?

A study conducted by Eccles, Barber, Stone, and Hunt (2003) investigated the connection between student participation in an extracurricular activity and adolescent development. The researchers conducted a longitudinal study of 1,800 students beginning in the sixth grade and concluding at the age of twenty-five or twenty-six. The researchers looked at five types of extracurricular activities, including prosocial activities, team sports, performing arts, school-involvement activities, and academic clubs. Overall, researchers found that participation in any of the five types of extracurricular activities promoted academic performance including high school GPA, college attendance, and college graduation.

They also found that in most cases extracurricular involvement helped to limit alcohol and drug use. The authors concluded:

> Involvement in a school organization or sport links an adolescent to a set of similar peers, provides shared experiences and goals,

and can reinforce friendships between peers and relationships with adults, particularly school personnel. Thus, extracurricular activities can facilitate adolescents' developmental needs for social relatedness, and can contribute to one's identity as an important and valued member of the school community. (Eccles et al., 2003, 874)

Students' identities and behaviors can be affected by involvement in an extracurricular activity.

In another study, researchers investigated student participation in youth activities. Hansen, Larson, and Dworkin (2003) used the Youth Experiences Survey to assess student experience in different activities. The researchers found that students participating in youth activities "reported more experiences related to personal development" (48) and "more frequent experiences reflecting interpersonal development" (49). Based on this research, it can be concluded that students involved in extracurricular activities can develop and explore aspects of their identity.

Overall, the research supports involvement in extracurricular activities as beneficial to students in many ways. Students may benefit by setting higher academic goals and avoiding substance abuse. Students also have opportunities to relate to peers and adults. In these situations, students' identities are molded and shaped.

Arts as Extracurricular Activities

Next, it is important to provide a rationale for the focus of arts as extracurricular activities. Numerous arts education theorists write about the importance of the arts as an experience and as curricula, but in today's world what has become more important is legislation. The United States passed No Child Left Behind (NCLB) in 2001. This comprehensive education legislation can be used as a rationale for inclusion of the arts.

In Title IX, Part A, Section 9101, NCLB defines core academic subjects. "The term 'core academic subjects' means English, reading or language arts, science, foreign languages, civics and government, economics, arts, history and geography" (NCLB, 2002).

According to recent legislation, the arts are now considered a core academic subject. For purposes of this discussion the arts will be considered extracurricular activities, but the fact that their role has been recast in the public school curricula supports the importance of the arts in schools.

Benefits of Participation in the Arts

Research has shown that student participation in any extracurricular activity will have an effect on his/her identity; participation in the arts is no exception. Many articles and organizations claim that participation in the arts will increase academic achievement for the student. According to Elliot Eisner (1999), arts educators frequently advertise the arts as a means to improving academic achievement with little research to back up the claim. While the argument over the connection of arts participation and academic achievement is interesting and worthwhile, the focus here will be on other benefits gained by students who participate in an extracurricular arts activity. Students who participate in arts activities may develop a positive self-concept, increase their multicultural awareness, and foster a sense of community.

Arts Participation and Student Identity

By definition the arts are a very personal experience. Merriam-Webster Online defines art as "the conscious use of skill and creative imagination especially in the production of aesthetic objects" (2003). Obviously a student's imagination is personal and distinctive. The process of art (creating and performing) and the arts experience (viewing and listening) cannot be separated from the individual's imagination. Each person holds within himself a unique creative power. That creative power must have an impact upon the type of person that student becomes and the ways they view themselves in the world environment.

Two major arts advocacy groups offer support for participation in the arts leading to a more positive self-concept for students. The President's Committee on the Arts and the Humanities and the

National Assembly of State Arts Agencies published a brochure titled *Eloquent Evidence: Arts at the Core of Learning* (1995) using material from the National Endowment for the Arts. According to the brochure, students who participated in the arts "reported significantly improved attitudes relating to self-expression, trust, self-acceptance," and they "derived satisfaction from their band experience regardless of their perceptions of their talents" (Murfee, 1995, 10). *Eloquent Evidence* (1995) also reports that a review of fifty-seven studies shows that self-concept was positively enhanced through arts participation.

In addition, a study conducted by James S. Catterall (1997) reported that students from economically disadvantaged backgrounds that were heavily involved in arts reported higher self-concepts than those students who were not involved as much. Both sources state that students who are actively involved with some arts activity can positively enhance their self-concept.

Research is not the only reason to connect arts participation with student identity. Professionals in the arts fields believe that self-discovery and personal reflection are at the heart of arts education. In a report on the conclusions of a think tank of professional theater artists, the International Center for the Study of Theatre Education, included a statement from the participants about the nature of educational theater. The panel said:

> Students should be encouraged to develop theatre which expresses their own experiences as well as integrates the experiences of others. Upon graduation from the educational system, through theatre, students should be able to successfully validate their own world outlook as well as understand the elements of other world outlooks. (Bedard, n.d., 43)

A journey of self-discovery is intrinsic to the arts experience. The Center for the Arts in the Basic Curriculum also acknowledges the connection between identity and arts participation. Stephanie Perrin (1997), writing for the Center for the Arts in the Basic Curriculum, shares observations of benefits for students. Students profit from the arts by developing a positive sense of self, imagination, cooperation, and productivity. Among arts educators and professional artists, there is an expectation of self-discovery from engaging in an artistic activity.

The experience of the arts gives students a chance to figure out who they are and what they find important. In all art forms, the participant must look at himself in order to create. An actor uses personal experiences as resources for characters. A visual artist recalls images and emotions to create a work of art. A musician must understand how a note can evoke feelings by the way it is played. Within all these processes, students examine their past experiences and determine what is important to them as a person. A young girl may discover she is interested in women's rights after performing in *Antigone*. Not only will she begin to understand what is important to her, but she will also be able to view the world from another perspective.

Arts Participation and Multicultural Awareness

Participation in the arts can also help students to widen their multicultural perspectives. Nearly all cultures have some form of arts. Music is said to be the universal language. There is no need for words to understand da Vinci's *Mona Lisa*. Elements of theater cross national boundaries and continents; a pratfall is funny anywhere. In the basic structure of any arts program are foundations of multicultural education. In a beginning drama class, students start learning about theater beginning with the Greek culture, then religious plays, and Shakespeare. The same holds true for other arts; all cultures have contributed to the arts. Educators can then take these opportunities for multicultural experiences and help students broaden their global perspectives.

Again there is support for using the arts to enhance students' multicultural awareness. Murfee (1995) also cites a study in Arizona where stereotypical views of Native Americans were diminished in elementary students through music education (1996). It makes sense to use the arts to understand different cultures and in turn increase tolerance.

In addition, the think tank from the International Center for the Study of Theatre Education included diversity in their credo:

> A comprehensive theatre curriculum will challenge students to engage with the multiplicity of forms of theatre from various ethnic cultures, encourage them to examine the diverse contexts from which these forms grow and evoke in them a positive curiosity about the diversity of human experiences as expressed through this art form. (Bedard, n.d., 43)

An integral part of the arts is the ability to look at experiences from different perspectives.

Not only can the arts be used to broaden the multicultural perspective of a student, but it can also be used to reach a wide variety of students. In her report for Center for the Arts in the Basic Curriculum, Perrin (1997) suggests that the arts can be used to reach students through different learning styles and multiple intelligences. Schools with arts programs offer a variety of ways for students to learn and develop their talents. She also states that arts programs can help diminish tensions between minority and majority groups, "a school where one can communicate by playing an instrument, singing, dancing, and painting is a school where there are many opportunities for all students to be seen in the fullest sense by their peers" (9). Students begin to view each other as artists rather than by superficial criteria. In turn, they relate to each other as people across cultures.

Participation in the arts allows students to experience other cultures through various forms like music and dance. Students can begin to understand the world from a perspective that is not their own. In addition, students can come together as peers, as artists, trying to accomplish a common artistic goal. The arts can be a critical factor in increasing multicultural awareness of students that allows them to place themselves in a global context.

Arts Participation and Sense of Community

The last factor for discussion is community. Students who participate in an extracurricular activity in the arts can gain a better sense of community and responsibility. As students struggle to find their own identity, they also fight to find a place in the world and the community. Artistic activities can provide a means for students to discover where they fit in the big picture.

Catterall (1997) discusses community in his research study for Americans for the Arts. He reports that students involved in the arts develop a sense of community and also value community service more than students with little or no involvement in the arts. He concludes:

> Many arts activities, particularly the performing arts, also promote community—advancing shared purpose and team spirit required to perform an ensemble musical or dramatic work, or to design and paint a public mural. With the promotion of community surely comes empathy and general attachment to the larger values of the school and the adult society which high school students will soon join. (9)

In another study, Brice Heath, Soep, and Roach (1998) found that young artists are four times more likely to perform community service. The arts students are also developing a sense of community and learning to work together and create a community of artists and, hopefully, will eventually extrapolate those skills to the larger global community.

Many schools reach out to other schools or community organizations to help facilitate or enhance arts programs. Students learn about their role in the community by acting as part of the community. High school music programs may offer a lunchtime jazz program at the junior high. The drama club may perform drug awareness plays to educate elementary students. After actively working in the school community, students can become active members of the larger community. Students in art at the middle school may volunteer to paint a mural over the graffiti on the downtown buildings. Extracurricular activities in the arts can lead students to develop a role in their school community as well as the larger community. These active roles can then in turn help students form a positive self-concept.

Beyond a Single Student's Identity

The major focus of this chapter has been the benefits that enhance a sense of identity in students from participation in the arts. It is also important to discuss larger implications of student involvement in the arts. Sleeter and Grant (2007) state dominant groups in society create an image of the minority group using many means, including the arts. The authors list examples where negative characteristics have been attributed to low socioeconomic groups, ethnic groups, and genders in movies, television, and art. These constructed identities of specific minority groups can only be shattered and reconstructed by participation in the very media used to create them.

Sleeter and Grant (2007) continue to say that the authentic identity of the group is represented in the films, books, and arts created by the members of that group. Greene (2000) also supports arts as a means for social change. As each student individually participates in the arts, he or she not only reaps the benefits of a clear sense of identity, a raised awareness of multicultural issues, a sense of belonging to a community, but also becomes an author of the identity of his or her group. As those students begin to collectively work with an arts experience, they also become agents of social change.

Implications for Schools and Stakeholders

So what does this mean for educators and schools? The arts as an extracurricular activity offer a means to approach students in different ways. There are practical applications for the use of the arts for teachers, students, and community.

First, teachers need to be aware that students participating in the arts have alternative ways to explore their identity than traditional means. Arts activities can help students decide who they are and help create a positive self-image based on success in the discipline. Teachers can support students in these efforts and encourage and guide students to participate in an artistic activity. Also, core curriculum teachers can offer artistic opportunities in their classes. Teachers also need to realize that participation in the arts can help students gain new perspectives. A class troubled with racial tension could benefit from an artistic challenge. Classroom teachers can also use the arts as a bridge to community involvement. Every educator need not be an arts teacher to see the benefits of arts participation.

Second, as stated previously, students have a great deal to gain personally from the arts, but as a group students can also benefit from arts involvement. If students are developing positive self-concepts, more global perspectives, and a greater sense of community, the student body will become more cohesive and less discontent. Students involved in arts activities have ample opportunities to socialize and grow.

The third aspect to benefit is community. As students grow and change, the community gains entertainment. All the recitals, productions, concerts, and showings offer the community a way to come together. In turn, the students gain the artistic experience.

Finally, students who participate in the arts can be empowered as agents for social change. They can create and share an identity that is an authentic, positive, and powerful representation of any ethnicity, religion, economic class, or other group to which they belong. As students refine and shape their identity through arts experience, teachers and administrators should be supportive and encourage a voice of social justice.

In conclusion, by no means are arts-based extracurricular activities a way to save all students or all schools. The arts are not a magic pill that can cure all the problems in our educational system today. In this discussion, several benefits for students were offered. Not all students will benefit in the same way and some students may gain little from the arts, but the option to participate should be available. This chapter should be read as an introduction to ways to enhance student identity, multicultural awareness, and sense of community through the extracurricular activities in the arts as well as a means to social change.

References

Bedard, R. L. (n.d.). *Perspectives on theatre literacy* (No. 1). Tempe, AZ: American Alliance for Theatre and Education.

Brice Heath, S., Soep, E., & Roach, A. (1998). Living the arts through language + learning: A report on community-based youth organizations. *Americans for the Arts Monographs, 2*(7), 1–20.

Catterall, J. S. (1997). Involvement in the arts and success in secondary school. *Americans for the Arts Monograph, 1*(9), 1–12.

Eccles, J. S., Barber, B. L., Stone, M., & Hunt, J. (2003). Extracurricular activities and adolescent development. *Journal of Social Issues, 59*(4), 865–89.

Eisner, E. W. (1999). Does experience in the arts boost achievement? *Clearing House, 72*(3), 143–49.

Greene, M. (2000). *Releasing imagination: Essays on education, the arts, and social change.* San Francisco: Jossey-Bass.

Hansen, D. M., Larson, R. W., & Dworkin, J. B. (2003). What adolescents learn in organized youth activities: A survey of self-reported developmental experiences. *Journal of Research on Adolescence, 13*(1), 25–55.

Merriam-Webster Online. (2003). *Merriam-Webster Online Dictionary.* Retrieved March 15, 2007, from www.m-w.com/cgi-bin/dictionary

Murfee, E. (1995). *Eloquent evidence: Arts at the core of learning.* Washington, DC: President's Committee on the Arts and Humanities.

Perrin, S. B. (1997). *Education through the arts in secondary schools.* Retrieved November 20, 2004, from www.newhorizons.org/ofc_cabcperrin@.html

Sleeter, C. E., & Grant, C. A. (2007). *Making choices for multicultural educations: Five approaches to race, class and gender.* Hoboken, NJ: Wiley & Sons.

U.S. Department of Education (2002). No Child Left Behind Act of 2001, H.R. 1 (S.R. 1), 107th Congress, 147 Cong. Rec. 1425 (2001). Retrieved May 15, 2004, from www.ed.gov/legislation/ESEA02/107-110.pdf

8

Recognition, Identity Politics, and the Special Needs Student

Sandra Stewart

Scenario: One Student's Story

As a former special education teacher and principal, but more important, parent of a child with a learning disability, I believed that my understanding of the social and emotional stigma placed on children with special needs had been all but extinguished (at least in my classroom, on my campus, and with my child). That was until a recent conversation with my child about this issue.

My daughter was not identified as a child with a learning disability in reading until ninth grade. Though we struggled to help her through during the elementary- and middle-school years, it became apparent that she was not going to pass one or more portions of the Texas Assessment of Academic Skills (TAAS), which was the state-mandated annual assessment required for graduating with a Texas high school diploma. Due to my background and understanding of laws and policies regarding special education services, I believed that my child would not only be able to graduate from high school, but would also benefit from special services; that the teachers would provide the instruction and support needed in order to help her grow and improve in all content areas. We even made sure that she was fully included in all regular classrooms, just with modifications.

To my surprise, my daughter's description of the reality of being identified with a learning disability and the social and emotional trauma that resulted from four years as a "labeled" student has caused me to reflect on my own beliefs and previous actions concerning children with special needs. Amanda stated that though she struggled throughout her schooling career, especially in middle school, she received much more help and support as a "regular" student than she ever did as a "special needs" student.

As an identified "dyslexic" 504 student, she received reading services from a reading specialist, tutoring from all of her teachers, and intensive individualized instruction in TAAS objectives prior to taking the tests. As a matter of fact, Amanda never failed a TAAS test until the eighth grade. It should be noted here that she does not look back on those experiences with fondness, primarily due to the fact that she missed out on many elective and extracurricular activities due to her academic struggles. However, her identity as an individual and the "perceived" attention she received from her teachers provided the needed emotional support in the school setting.

It was at the point in which she was identified, or, as she terms it, "labeled," that the stigma and isolation from being identified as a student with a learning disability dramatically impacted her self-esteem and her "identity" as a high school student with peers, school personnel, and within herself. She expressed the feeling that she went from being recognized as a student with needs, primarily from her teachers, to a feeling that she was invisible in the regular classroom.

High school became a place of, as she put it, "ashamedness," especially given the fact that both of her parents were principals and her sister was academically at the top of her class. Prior to being identified, she had more attention than she wanted from her teachers and school specialists. After she was identified, all of that went away, creating within her a feeling of isolation and invisibility in the classroom. Teachers now focused their attention on other students in the classroom.

While being fully included in the regular education classroom, her teachers provided little or no instruction on her level. As a matter of fact, one of two "teacher actions" now took place in the classroom. There were the teachers who modified her work or her workload and gave her more time to finish assignments, but with little or no help in the content on her level. Then there were those who would not modify the work at her level, but rather had her struggle and fail her daily assignments and tests, and then would "give" her a 70 on her report card.

As a parent, special education teacher, and public school administrator, my own feelings tainted my ability to "see" what she was experiencing, especially since she complied with testing so that she would not have to face the disgrace of failing another standardized assessment. We sincerely believed that we were doing what was best for her in the given situation by trying to take some of the academic pressure off of her. Instead we created an emotional trauma in which Amanda felt unworthy and unimportant.

This scenario might have been a fictional portrayal designed to provide a setting for this paper; however, it is not fictional, but rather factual and personal. This case provides the backdrop for this chapter in order to draw attention to issues related not only to the importance of academic success, but also how a loss of recognition and identity can negatively impact the ability of a student with special needs to even progress academically.

Some questions to be considered throughout this chapter will be: Do certain identity groups denote a negative perception by society and educational stakeholders? Do educational leaders and principals, in particular, have a responsibility in forming the culture of campus perceptions by staff, students, parents, and community; or does society have such an impact on the culture of the identity of groups within the educational system that leaders do not impact those perceptions? How do these perceptions attribute to the success of "identified" groups of students—in particular, students identified with special needs, and the academic, social, and emotional success of students in the public school setting? Do well-intentioned educators, desiring to help students become academically successful, set special needs students up for failure in the

social, emotional, and academic setting of today's high-stakes educational setting?

All of these questions raise serious concerns about how we
teach, learn, and how people's identities, and more specifically,
"identity group" impact the experiences that students carry with
them throughout their educational careers, and more important,
their places as contributing citizens in a democratic society. How
can we promote democracy in which the people participate in the
decision-making process, if some are excluded from the "group"?
Simpson, Jackson, Bunuan, Yoke-Meng Chan, Collins, King, and
Mosley (2003–2004) indicate that ethical educators realize that
present students will be the future of society and that educational
leaders must promote high expectations for all when they state,
"Believing that every child deserves both respect and an appropriate high quality education, that the health and progress of society
partially depends upon the school striving for democratic ideas"
(81).

This chapter is designed to challenge the current ways in which
educational leaders and teachers perceive the importance of recognition and identity in developing academic learning for students
with special needs. This chapter will first define the terms "recognition," "identity," "group identity," and "cultural identity." An
understanding of the student "identification" process and the impact of "labeling" for special education will then be considered.
Next, the concept of "group identity" and its affect on campus culture, and the beliefs and actions of leadership, teachers, and students will be considered. Finally, this chapter will consider how
educational leaders and principals can implement a campus vision,
goals and objectives, professional development, and high expectations for teacher actions and student success by developing a "campus identity" that recognizes and celebrates the talents and abilities
of all students.

Defining Terms

Merriam-Webster's dictionary (2007) defines identity as "the dis-
tinguishing character or personality of a human being." This defi-

nition would indicate a person's identity is demonstrated through character actions and personality, thus being portrayed by the individual self. In essence, the individual's actions and character define his identity. According to Appiah (2005), the actions and behaviors of an individual shape their identity. If an individual exhibits actions, characteristics, and beliefs that others identify with, then others' recognition of that individual can be internalized and thus become a part of his identity. Taylor (1989) suggests that people's identity is formed from what is deemed "good" and acceptable in the community and social settings in which the person is associated.

Recognition is defined as "the action of recognizing or the state of being recognized or acknowledged, or special notice or attention" (Merriam-Webster's dictionary, 2007). This definition lies within others' perceptions or recognition of a person. People then can have control over the recognition of others. This recognition can then be translated into the person's identity. Bingham (2001) bases his understanding of how recognition from others affects the identity of the person: "The self, according to this call for recognition, is not autonomously situated. Instead, the self always looks to others for its sense of identity" (61). If, then, a person's identity is influenced by others recognition of that identity, how are students identified with special needs shaped by educators' and peers' perceptions of the "group identity" of students with disabilities and their ability and expectations for learning?

If individual identity is based on the personality and actions of the person being identified with, then how does the association of a particular group influence the individual's identity? Can a group possess an identity? According to Webster's dictionary (2007), a group is defined as "a number of individuals that are unified in a common unit." Therefore, group identity is based on the actions and characteristics of a number of individuals that are unified for a common purpose.

Individuals can purposefully join themselves into a group or they can, by default, become part of a group. For example, a person can join the Key Club and voluntarily become a part of the group. This group is identified by their actions and associations with others outside the group. If this same person is accused of a crime, then she becomes associated with the legal system by default. In the educational system, students are automatically a part of many groups: school, classroom, lunch group, and identified programs. Students identified with a disability become part of an exclusive group impacted by the perceptions of the cultural identity associated with special needs.

Sergiovanni (1996) defines school culture as "what people believe, the assumptions they make about how schools work, and what they consider to be true and real" (3). The school culture is formed through its actions and belief systems, thus its identity. Cultural identity of the school is recognized through the actions or lack of actions of the people in the learning community based on the professed beliefs and assumptions espoused by the school. It should be noted that a school cannot exist without an identity, whether the identity is positive or negative. All schools profess and advocate beliefs about students and learning. Whether the people in the group act upon those beliefs or not determines the school's cultural identity.

Identity, recognition, group identity, and cultural identity shape the learning community, the people associated in the learning community, and the success of the school, staff, and students. I will refer to these definitions in an effort to explain how they specifically influence the beliefs of principals, teachers, and students who have been identified as special needs students.

Identifying and Identity of Students with Disabilities

Since the beginning of public education, serving children with disabilities or special needs has been the proving ground for much debate. The laws and policies that govern special services for children with disabilities was, from the outset, focused on providing instruction and services that would aid students, to the greatest extent possible, to live and work productively as adults. Much emphasis, in the beginning, attended to the severe and profound disabilities—physical impairments, chromosomal disorders (Down syndrome), and severe mental disorders—in an effort to bring respect and "identity" to students that suffered from these disorders. As with all laws and policies, identification, assessments, and services have evolved in the public school arena.

Though for the purposes of this chapter, it is not necessary to examine the history of special education services in public education, a review of the law that governs the identification and services pertaining to students in public education that qualify for special education services will add to the understanding of how identity and recognition affect these students.

In 1975, Public Law 94-142 was passed mandating fair and appropriate educational services for all children with disabilities or suspected disabilities. Since that time, many changes and updates to this law have been implemented (Kallio & Geisel, 2005). The Individuals with Disabilities Education Act (IDEA) is the federal law that governs public schools today. Though the federal law mandates services in public schools, states are responsible for the identification and services provided in public schools. Therefore, the criteria and timelines may be different from state to state. Where states typically differ is not with providing services for the severe and profound, but rather those that qualify as learning disabled students.

The majority of children with severe and profound disabilities have one or more physical characteristics that identify that disability. Many of these children are receiving state services before entering public school. Early childhood education special services begin in the public school system at the age of three (Kallio & Geisel, 2005). Systems are already in place for these children upon entering public school. Therefore, the concepts of identity and recognition have been in place for these children from birth. In other words, their disability has always helped to define their "identity." They were recognized by their disability in the community and home before entering the schoolhouse.

All students, no matter the severity of the disability, should be treated with respect and should be recognized as an individual, not a collective "labeled" group. The majority of students identified with a severe or profound disability are place in a self-contained special needs classroom for the majority of the day. Many students with these severe disabilities are provided social time in the regular education classroom or time, through lunch and recess, to spend with typical students.

Though it is necessary for the physical well being of students with severe disabilities to receive specific and intense instruction and services from trained professionals in a self-contained room, the physical isolation from typical peers sends an underlying message to those peers that "those people" are not part of the mainstream and thus exclusion is not only necessary, but also desired. How then can students with severe and profound disabilities be recognized by the mainstream as contributing participants?

Educators tend to sell children short when it comes to understanding the emotional and social needs of children with severe disabilities. After all, how can educators teach or model respect and positive recognition for children with severe disabilities if they do not believe that they are just as responsible for the success of children with disabilities as they are for the typical students in their classroom? All teachers, regular and special education, must work in harmony to create a positive atmosphere for acceptance and expectation for students with profound disabilities.

Providing instruction and opportunities for typical peers to study and work with the profoundly disabled creates an understanding and caring attitude that supports the academic, social, and emotional growth of all children. IDEA has provided the laws and policies governing the rights of students with disabilities. Though laws can mandate services for students identified with one or more learning disabilities, the law cannot mandate educator perceptions, high expectations, and fair and ethical treatment in the classroom.

Due to the physical traits of most students with severe and profound disabilities, their identities are part of their disabilities. Therefore, what can be seen can be addressed. No one disputes the intentions or motivation of these students; however, that is not the case with students identified while in school and with a learning disability that is not "seen." Typically, students with learning disabilities are not identified until they have been taught in the regular classroom setting for two or more years. Therefore, students with learning disabilities enter school with an identity that has already been established at home and will be influenced by the experiences in each of the classrooms from year to year.

The process for identifying a student with a learning disability takes many years. After a child has been exposed to and had the same opportunities for learning as their typical peers, students that are not performing academically on grade level begin a process of referral for special education. Most states require that the school system provide intensive supports in the regular education classroom before referring a child for special services. These requirements differ from state to state but are required to document all interventions prior to referral (Kallio & Geisel, 2005). The purpose behind this process is to ensure that children are not misplaced in the system.

All students are developmentally on different levels when entering school, due to prior experiences, age, and developmental maturity. After all regular options have been exhausted, the referral system begins. Students referred for testing due to academic learning concerns have been struggling in the regular classroom for at least a couple of years. By this time, the child is probably frustrated, as are the teachers, and emotionally defeated.

According to Sprenger (1999), emotions and self-esteem directly impact the ability of people to learn. The frontal lobe of the brain, which processes learning, can be blocked by emotional stressors. Therefore, students who become stressed because they are not able to understand or keep up with the pace of the learning environment are actually perpetuating the problem of learning. This emotional distress can also create behavioral issues, either acting out or withdrawing.

As the child's identity is beginning to be shaped by his experiences in the school setting, the recognition by teachers has been primarily negative, not necessarily on purpose but by the circumstances of learning expectations in the classroom. Consequently, the child internalizes these negative experiences, which are manifested in his identity. Appiah (2005) states that an individual's identity is shaped by their actions and behaviors: "What I do intentionally is dependent on what I think I am doing" (65).

Once a child qualifies and is identified with a learning disability, a number of options can take place. Based on the needs of the individual child, a number of plans can be created in the Admissions, Review, and Dismissal (ARD) meeting. During an ARD, the administrator, testing specialist, regular education teacher, special education teacher, and parent make decisions for special services in order to best serve the academic needs of the child. IDEA requires at the time of planning that the child must be provided a plan that considers Least Restrictive Environment (LRE) (Kallio & Geisel, 2005). This means that the ARD must first consider instruction with modifications in the regular education classroom. Based on these needs, other services can be added until a plan that is conducive to the individual needs of the student has been developed.

This plan is a legally binding document requiring all stake-holders to ensure that the needs of the child are met so that the child can grow academically (Kallio & Geisel, 2005). The ultimate goal of the ARD is eventually to be able to dismiss the child from receiving special services. In actuality, this rarely happens. Once the ARD plan is complete, implementation of it must begin. Unfortunately, too many times an assumption is made that any social and emotional issues stemming from the lack of success in the regular classroom will "fix" itself once the academic pressure is off the child. The fallacy in this assumption is that there will be no emotional "fallout" from the stigma of being labeled a child with special needs.

It would seem logical that by meeting the academic needs of the student on his/her level and providing opportunities for academic success, the emotional aspect of nonsuccess would dissipate. However, two aspects must be considered. First, the child will not begin to feel academically successful for a period of time, and second, the child now must sort through emotions of feeling "different" and being "not accepted" as a regular peer in the classroom and may have one or more new teachers now. In addition, if the teacher begins recognizing the student as a special needs student instead of an individual, then the identity crisis takes on a new dynamic. It is the moral and ethical responsibility of the principal and teacher or teachers to consider these issues and make a plan to meet these emotional needs as well as the academic.

Again, teachers do not need to underestimate the ability of children to know and understand "difference." As a matter of fact, teachers who celebrate diversity and difference in the classroom and principals who embrace differences on the campus can alleviate many of these issues from the outset. Educators who model and teach that all people are individual and different and unique, and that we all have different strengths and must rely on one another to help us grow, will, by default, instill recognition for difference that will positively shape each child's identity.

IDEA is the law in place that provides the provisions for identifying and implementing special services for students with disabilities. Children born with disabilities enroll in public school with identities that have already been shaped by their limitations, which create for a smoother transition in the school setting. However, ethical educators will recognize individual students, even with severe disabilities, for their uniqueness and contribution to the learning community. This will not only aid in moving from low expectations for learning, but also will help typical students to understand and accept difference positively.

Students that are identified with learning disabilities after a few years in the educational system must have their individual identities protected and support systems put in place to help them cope with the emotional changes that will take place. It is imperative that educators recognize all students for their differences and create opportunities to recognize the successes of individuals and the classroom so that each student can feel secure in their identity and that positive group identities can be formed.

Group Identity

One's identity is not just related to self; rather, it is shaped by the groups we identify with and have intimate association. Group identity is not a new concept. People have a natural instinct to be grouped with others that have common interests or goals as themselves. Group identity is dependent on the actions and perceptions built around those groups. These groups are identified, not only by their actions, but more important, by the perceptions of people outside the group.

Consider the high school student who participates in football, University Interscholastic League (UIL), and the Spanish club is identified as an individual and a member of these groups. Based on the perceptions of these groups, this individual may be recognized positively or negatively by others for his accomplishments. If the football team wins a state championship, then even if he does not play during the championship game, he is identified with the team and thus being a part of the group was a positive experience. At the same time, if some of the members of the Spanish Club are suspended for inappropriate actions during a meeting, even if he were not in the meeting, his group identity is negatively impacted. How does the association of being identified as a student with special needs affect the identity of the student? How do the actions of educators and peers impact the identity of the student receiving special services?

Students identified with special needs are labeled with one or more disabilities in order to receive services, services intended to positively impact the student's learning and cognitive growth. In addition to receiving individualized services, a student's label automatically qualifies him with the special education group identity in which he is now recognized. The very idea of special education assumes a negative connotation in the public school arena, due to a qualification of a person with a disability.

A person with a disability is one that: "(i) has a physical or mental impairment, which substantially limits one or more major life activities, (ii) has a record of such an impairment, or (iii) is regarded as having such an impairment" (Americans with Disabilities, 2006, §104.3(j)(1)). Therefore, a student with a disability is negatively perceived by others due to the having an "impairment." Schools do not identify students for special education until all other options are extinguished. Can students identified with special needs be positively impacted if the group identity does not connote positive association by teachers, administrators, and peers?

Society is shaped by how people identify themselves and their groups. Therefore, people are not only recognized by the people around them, but also the recognition received determines the identity of the person and impacts their competence and participation in the societal setting. Consequently, the stigma experienced by students with disabilities can impair their ability to participate in other positive groups in the educational setting.

Take, for example, the story of my daughter. Amanda was excluded from some positive groups in the school setting due to her disability. Though she could participate in some activities, they were limited due to intense tutoring and the "extra" time needed by the school to provide that intense academic teaching. Consequently, the groups that could have provided more opportunity for Amanda to be positively recognized were not options for her.

This negative perception does not indicate that teachers, administrators, and peers do not care about students with special needs; rather educators make conclusions about the individual student based more on the "disability" label instead of their individual attributes. Therefore, group identity impacts perceptions of the student's abilities and expectations for success in the school setting. Consequently, students with a disability lose their individual identity and become part of the group identity.

Ironically, IDEA supports and even mandates that educators consider the individual needs of the child by developing an Individual Education Plan (IEP) for each student (Kallio & Geisel, 2005). The purpose behind the IEP is to consider all individual aspects and needs of the student in an effort to keep the group mentality from negatively affecting the student with a special need.

Though some principals and teachers do not demonstrate a caring for special needs students, the majority of educators are caring and sensitive to their needs; however, the perception of a disability is observed in the expectations for student success. As stated earlier, most educators are passionate and caring people striving to provide instruction that will assist students in improved academic achievement. However, special education, by definition, carries with it a stigma of difference from typical peers. Therefore, educators, even special education teachers, the primary supporters of students with special needs, understand that this group, though exclusive, is not a desired one in which to be associated.

Group identity impacts all humans in that they are recognized through every association they have as humans. People are grouped by their jobs, their churches, their clubs, and so forth. How people perceive their own identities and the identity of the groups they associate with affect their perceptions of themselves. In turn, how people recognize others is primarily based on the identity of the groups in which they have association, either positively or negatively. How, then, do socially just and caring principals and educational leaders promote positive group identity of students with special needs? Can campus culture envelope beliefs that can change the negative association of students being labeled with a disability?

Principal Responsibility to Campus Identity

The role and responsibility of principals and educational leaders have shifted over the past two decades. In the past, principals were subject to controlling or managing the educational setting in order to manage people, the budget, and facilities so that teachers could provide instruction for the students. This philosophy, based on Frederick Taylor's Scientific Management Theory, was a prevalent doctrine that was the foundation for the principal's leadership. With the progress of public education and a focus on ensuring the academic, social, and emotional success for each individual student and a new vision promoting educational leadership instead of educational management, future prospects look bright—for most.

A socially just, democratic system entitles all students to receive the best educational teaching staff, educational leaders, and curriculum designed to ensure success for each individual. How the principal or educational leader communicates these values and beliefs to the staff that will transfer them into meaningful change in attitudes and beliefs has been focus in the educational arena for the past decade. Many books and journals have been written on how principals affect change in an ever-changing educational system. Harris (2004) explains that change is about people, not programs, and that effective change happens when the principal focuses on individuals.

In addition to the promotion of high expectations for success, principals and educational leaders must provide a positive culture of identity focused on staff as well as students. When the principal is recognized as one that emulates an ability to provide successful leadership and confidence in the system, teachers will then internalize this philosophy and identity of confidence in their abilities to ensure success for themselves and all of their students. Fullen (2001) terms this process as "reculturing." He states, "Transforming the culture—changing the way we do things around here—is the main point" (44).

Ultimately, passionate, ethical, and moral principals and educational leaders can make a difference by sharing a vision that encourages individual successes and opportunities for all students to identify and contribute as a productive member of a community of learners. According to Jenlink (2003–2004), socially just leaders understand that they "affect just and democratic practices that foster conditions necessary to self-identity and self-respect, self-development and self-expression, and self-determination and self-democratization" (9). When the individuals in the school community understand their roles and responsibilities to the group, these attitudes become entrenched in the culture of the school.

Principals can provide the leadership necessary to make meaningful changes that will promote student success and, in turn, assist teachers and students in internalizing a positive identity that will lead to an increased confidence in teachers' abilities to teach and students' abilities and willingness to learn. Fullen (2001) explains that principals and educational leaders contribute to what he terms "moral purpose," even if the leader is unaware of this phenomenon. He further states that these beliefs can be taught and passed on purposefully to staff and students and is evident in the culture of the campus; therefore, it is vital to verbalize these beliefs and expected actions collaboratively. This would indicate then that principals can purposefully create a positive culture that promotes positive identity based on individual strengths and acceptance.

Though this chapter has focused primarily on students with learning disabilities that spend a majority of school time with their typical peers, promoting a climate that supports expected success for students with the most severe disabilities is an important aspect for encouraging recognition of all students and cultural identity. How can educators proclaim social justice and democracy, and then isolate some from the system? If our purpose is to successfully educate people to become contributing citizens who give back to society, then principals must promote a culture that identifies with and recognizes the needs of all (McFadden et al, 2006).

One significant way in which educational leaders and principals create and promote this culture of acceptance is through professional development. If these beliefs and precepts can be taught, then leaders are responsible for ensuring this professional development. According to McFadden and colleagues (2006), principals must first be taught how to promote these issues and then provide professional development to the staff. Gallego, Hollingsworth, and Whitenack (2001) further state that collaboration among teachers sustains professional development and, in turn, the beliefs and instructional strategies are embedded into the culture of the campus.

Professional development is crucial in creating an identity culture that recognizes successes for students and staff. McFadden and colleagues (2006) suggest that the principal, as well as teachers, participate in professional development of special needs students. How can a community of learners be valid if the staff does not understand the basics of teaching children with special needs so that they can be successful?

In addition to providing professional development, principals must challenge teachers to consider and contemplate the question: What is intelligence? The community, as well as the educational system, must be informed in how to identify and build on student's individual intelligences. Amanda, though creative and bright, was a product of a system in which the area of intelligence in which she excelled was used as a reward system for passing the high-stakes standardized state assessment. Students not passing these assessments were placed in tutorials or small group instructional settings in place of the fine arts activities in which many of these students excelled, thus peeling away at their individual identities that make them special and unique and, instead, promoting the group identity and labeling system in which we placed them to promote a confidence in the learning process.

Harris (2004) advocates that principals model respectful treatment for all students and staff. Building relationships that value others and their contributions to the campus community strengthen the learning environment and success for all students and staff. When principals recognize these contributions, both privately and publicly, of students and staff, an expectation for teachers to do the same in their classroom is set: "To build relationships with actions that value others, principals must be fair, they must be caring, and they must acknowledge and celebrate diversity. In short, they must treat all people in ways that make them feel important" (Harris, 2004, 43).

Principals seeking to create a cultural identity of community for the campus must first understand the difference between the school as an organization and the school as a community. In the past, principals managed schools through budget allocations, facilities upkeep, student discipline, and school safety. This management system was designed around the concept of the CEO managing an organization. Though these components remain important responsibilities related to the position of principal or instructional leader, they are not the impetus for school success. On the other hand, communities are built around the social structures and relationships of the people (Sergiovanni, 1996). Communities focus on the people and lead through the beliefs and values of the campus. Communities then recognize the accomplishments and successes of all of the people that are embedded in the culture of the campus.

Harris (2004) suggests that principals ensure that all students have the opportunity to experience success and challenge teachers to learn more about their coworkers and students. This personal relationship creates a recognition of individuals that does not have to be directly related to traditional academic successes. Gallego, Hollingsworth, and Whitnack (2001) explain that in efforts to reform school cultures focused on student success, principals must know and create relationships with the staff and students.

Principals, creating a community that values and recognizes the successes of all by providing staff development, challenging the thinking about intelligence, building relationships, and then embedding these actions and beliefs in the culture of the campus, create a positive cultural identity in which all students and staff are recognized. The underlying questions principals must reflect on are "Can the negative connotation associated with being identified with a disability ever be turned into a positive?" and "How can changes in the cultural identity of campus influence the group identity associated with special education?"

Conclusion

A socially just and democratic educational system, by definition, substantiates the identity of each individual's talents, academic abilities, social and emotional contributions to peers, and ultimately the opportunity to contribute back to the community and society as a whole. In what was, from the beginning, a system set in place to improve the educational setting for students who had various learning and emotional disabilities, special education has, in fact, contributed to a backlash of low expectations for success.

The future of this country and the international community rely on the public school system to educate students so that they are prepared to contribute, as individuals, to a democratic society that celebrates individual identity, resulting in a diverse and productive society. Jenlink (2003–2004) indicates that "social justice and democracy are central to transforming society and creating a more democratic society based on diversity through democratic processes populated by individuals that represent diversity" (6). How have we accomplished this goal? Are we producing individuals with the tools needed to ensure a socially just and democratic community and world? Do educational leaders and teachers recognize and value the contributions of individuals with special needs in the global society, and more important, what is the impact of special needs students whose only identity has been one established through a "negative group identity"? We must consider how identity impacts the individual, the culture of a campus, and the future of our country and world. Principals of the future envision the school as a minicommunity, modeling, on a smaller scale, social justice, democracy, and a society of individuals prepared to collaborate productively in order to continue the values that established and founded this country and our world.

My daughter graduated from high school and now struggles with her identity as a contributing citizen. Though bright and highly creative, her confidence for success has been stifled by an educational system that, though well-intended, demonstrated complacency and nonexpectation for my daughter and her identified group of students with special needs. As stated throughout this chapter, what is intended and what is communicated many times can be quite different.

Special education teachers are normally caring and devoted educators striving to provide students with individualized instruction so that each can be successful and progress at their own rate. Regular education teachers, overwhelmed and overburdened many times, feel inept and unprepared for teaching to the levels that are dictated by No Child Left Behind (NCLB) legislation and the states' accountability systems. Under this pressure, teachers in regular education classrooms rely on special education teachers to "provide instruction" for children with special needs and tend to internalize their role and responsibilities for inclusion of students with special needs from a social and emotional aspect.

It is then the role and responsibility of the principal or educational leader to develop a collaborative vision that promotes beliefs of learning for all staff and students, communicate high expectations for learning, provide staff development that promotes success for all students, and recognize all staff and students for their successes. In short, the principal, teachers, and students practice what they say they believe.

References

Americans with Disabilities (2006). *How does ADA define disability?* Retrieved November 22, 2007, from dhfs.wisconsin.gov/disabilities/physical/definition.htm

Appiah, K. A. (2005). *Ethics of identity.* New York: Princeton University Press.

Bingham, C. W. (2001). *Schools of recognition: Identity politics and classroom practices.* New York: Rowman & Littlefield Publishers.

Fullen, M. (2001). *Leading in a culture of change.* San Francisco: Jossey-Bass Publishing.

Gallego, M. A., Hollingsworth, S., & Whitenack, D. A., (2001). Relational knowing in the reform of educational cultures. *Teacher College Record, 103*(2), 240–66.

Harris, S. (2004). *Bravo principal! Building relationships with actions that value others.* Larchmant, NY: Eye on Education.

Jenlink, P. (2003–2004). A scholar-practitioner stance: Practices of social justice and democracy. *Scholar-Practitioner Quarterly, 2*(2), 3–12.

Kallio, B. R., & Geisel, R. T. (2005). Special education. In A. P. Pankake, M. Littleton, & G. Schroth (Eds.), *The administration & supervision of special programs in education* (Second Ed.) Dubuque, IA: Kendall/Hunt Publishing Co.

McFadden, C. C., Colaric, S. M., Buckner, K., Kilburn, R., Sugar, W., & Warren, S. (2006). Professional development modules for school administrators: A tool for creating and sustaining supportive school cultures for all students. *School Leadership Review, 2*(1), 97–105.

Merriam-Webster's Dictionary. (2007). Retrieved December 20, 2007, from www.m-w.com/

Sergiovanni, T. J. (1996). *Leadership for the schoolhouse: How is it different? Why is it important?* San Francisco: Jossey-Bass Publishing.

Simpson, D. J., Jackson, M. J. B., Bunuan, R. L., Yoke-Meng Chan, B., Collins, R., King, E. L., & Mosley, L. K. (2003–2004). Toward a democratic ethic of curricular decision-making: A guide for educational practitioners. *Scholar-Practitioner Quarterly, 2*(2), 79–88.

Sprenger, M. (1999). *Learning and memory: The brain in action.* Alexandria, VA: Association for Supervision and Curriculum Development.

Taylor, C. (1989). *Sources of self: The making of modern identity.* Cambridge, MA: Harvard College Press.

9

Athletes, Recognition, and the Formation of Identity

Vincent E. Mumford

> With all due respect . . . when's the last time fifty thou-
> sand people showed up to watch a kid take a fucking
> chemistry test?
>
> James Caan as Coach Winters in *The Program*

Education is the cornerstone of American society. The educational system in the United States has been credited with much of the nation's successes—receiving praise for everything from the thriving U.S. economy to the country's technological superiority. The link of education and success in the United States is so inextricably intertwined that all children living in the United States have the right to a free public education, and all states have compulsory school attendance laws (U.S. Department of Education, 2001).

The system of a free public education has been idealistically considered by many to be the great equalizer of American society (Bennett, 1998). This romantic notion of what the role of U.S. education should be was first reflected upon by Horace Mann, known as the "Father of American Education" when he stated:

> Education, then, beyond all other devices of human origin, is the
> great equalizer of the conditions of men, the balance wheel of the
> social machinery. . . . It does better than to disarm the poor of their
> hostility toward the rich; it prevents being poor. (Messerli, 1972)

A free public education is viewed as the means to an end for all students. Indeed, public education is a vehicle that helps students to improve their lot in life. If one goes to school and works hard, success is considered almost a guaranteed by-product. Viewed in this context of benefits based on the values of hard work and determination, education is seen as the pathway to the American dream for all students.

Sports play a major role in American society and especially American education because of the values associated with participation. Sports and education have come to be so interlinked over the years because of these American values that the important impact of sports on American society has been recognized by the U.S. government. The fact that sports and participating in sport activities help individuals develop character, discipline, confidence, self-esteem, better health, and a sense of well-being was especially recognized by President Theodore Roosevelt and many presidents since (Guttman, 1991). Sports hold such a prominent place in our society that each year the president invites individual athletes or entire teams to visit the White House to be recognized by the most powerful individual in the free world.

Harvey Lauer (2002) echoed the sentiments that sports serve an important societal function when he stated, "It has been observed that after religion, sport is the most powerful cultural force in American society" (n.p.). We have learned from history that such powerful cultural forces, if left unexamined, can quickly occupy a position of cult status and ultimately do more harm than good. The enduring value of sports is that it is seen as a true meritocracy and like education, hard work, and determination, is a key to success rather than social position and socioeconomic status.

Scholastic sports are a privilege unique to American education, unique in what it does for schools, kids, and communities. Sports bring recognition to schools from the media. Kids who show promise in sports can receive athletic scholarships for college. For communities, sports can be a civic enterprise that brings the community together.

There has been very limited research or serious debate dealing with how student-athletes are recognized in the public space of schools (Taylor, 1999). Serious scholarly inquiry must inevitably ask the question whether the importance of sports in our culture is a good thing. Given all of the benefits attributed to sports participation, are we now nearing a time when success in sport at the scholastic level can make education seem unimportant? Put another way, are sports viewed as more important to student-athletes than chemistry?

While it is clear that the benefits obtainable through sports in an educational setting have value to all children, it is also clear that we must reexamine the relationship between sports and schools. Although the roles and status that each occupied was very clear with the Mature and the Baby Boomer generations, that line is beginning to blur with the Generation X and Millennial generations. According to Lapchick (1987–1988), we live in a sports-crazed society that is starting to emphasize athletics over education. This emphasis is in direct conflict with such evident functions of the school as promoting academic excellence, transmitting knowledge, and fostering the psychological and social development of the student (Goldberg & Chandler, 1989).

Identity and Sports

One of the most important challenges facing students today is the establishment of a sense of identity. The process of identity formation occurs throughout the course of one's life, with considerable strides being made during the school-age years (Chickering & Reisser, 1993).

A big part of the identity of the student-athlete is formed in the school setting. They spend hours upon hours practicing their sport and honing their skills for extracurricular activities. They interact with teachers, coaches, friends, and the media. Thus, the self-identity of the student-athlete is not determined by an enduring set of conferred characteristics, but through social interactions in various changing social roles and relationships.

Through this assortment of interactions and relationships, student-athletes develop an athletic identity. Athletic identity has been described as "the degree to which an individual identifies with the athletic role" (Brewer, Van Raalte, & Linder, 1993). Presumably, this same definition applies to any role we assume such that our "teacher identity" is the degree to which we identify with our role as a teacher, our "coach identity" is the degree to which we identify with our role as a coach, and so on. Sociologists refer to these images of oneself in particular role situations as "situated identities" (Ryska, 2002).

Athletic identity is different than other student identities. Athletic identity holds a unique status among other situated identities in the school setting. Being a student-athlete is akin to being a superhero, that is, the student-athlete has two identities. Readers of comic books are keenly aware that most superheroes have two identities: a secret identity and a superhero identity. By comparison, student-athletes have the "student" identity and the "athlete" identity. These two identities are often at odds with each other. For the student-athlete, the athletic identity is often more important than the student identity (Williams & Anderson, 1987).

For many boys in high school, being an athlete is the role they desire most. They would much rather be a star athlete than a brilliant student (Kane, 1988; Thirer & Wright, 1985; Williams & Andersen, 1987; Williams & White, 1983). Not only is being an athlete highly important to students in terms of status and popularity, student-athletes see the athlete role as a central and extremely important dimension of their self-concept. This view of looking at themselves as athletes influences everything from social relationships to types of activities sought, to perceptions of life experiences (Brewer, Van Raalte, & Linder, 1993). Indeed, students choose to participate in activities that are consistent with more highly developed and central aspects of their self-concept, and they likely will be more satisfied with relationships that may confirm or validate important dimensions of their self-concept (Cornelius, 1995).

Separate and Unequal Sports Identity

The student-athlete is not the normal student. Because of their participation in sports, they are recognized differently within the public space of schools. The athletic identity serves as a partition that separates and distinguishes them from their fellow classmates. Although student-athletes have the same obligations and rules to follow as those students who are not athletes, they are viewed much differently than the academic honor student, the band student, or the student body president. This social stratification takes the athlete out of the role of a student and puts him or her into a different role. The student-athlete is recognized as being different and thus is isolated and separated from his or her peers.

This separation and isolation begins early. Athletic identity is typically formed early in the child's life. Athletic talent is often recognized as early as elementary school. For many children (though certainly not all), developing that talent becomes a central preoccupation for both the child and the significant adults in his or her life. For those children, the time and psychological commitment to the role of athlete is such that by the time they reach high school, highly successful athletes have internalized the athletic identity, frequently at the expense of other possible social roles (e.g., academic honor student, band student, or student body president). These athletes are often put on a pedestal by teachers, coaches, friends, and the community in which they live. As a result, an internalized athlete identity likely dominates the individual's overall self-concept, and causes damage to the student or academic identity.

Many researchers fear that the system currently being emphasized in our schools of peer and community values built around the success of athletics may act as a detriment to academic achievement (Edwards, 2000; Lapchick, 1987–1988; Lumpkin, Stoll, & Beller, 2003; Snyder, 1985). When the student conforms fully or adequately to the athletic identity, he or she often does so at the expense of the student or academic identity. Eventually, a conflict develops between the two roles of student and athlete (Goldberg, 1991; Lapchick, 1987–1988).

148 / Chapter 9

Public Recognition and Sports

Although schools are a public space (Bingham, 2001), the recognition given to the normal student is much different than the recognition given to the student-athlete in that public space. The unique public nature of the athletic identity leads many to consider the student-athlete a public figure. Performing one's role as an athlete carries a visibility unlike most other role enactments in the school setting.

Athletic performances are typically displayed to a wider public audience than most role enactments. Most athletic competitions take place in gymnasiums or on fields, spaces much larger than the size of a normal school classroom. In addition, family, friends, fans, and other spectators usually come to watch the competition. Cheerleaders cheer for the home team, bands play the school fight song, and fans root for their favorite team. Schools often go out of their way to recognize athletic competition. In doing so, schools demonstrate the real value placed on athletic competition.

The example of Lebron James will serve to illustrate this point. James was one of the most highly recognized and most highly publicized high school athletes ever when he was a senior at Vincent–St. Mary High School in Akron, Ohio. Because of the recognition he received for being a star athlete, his school's home games were moved from the small gymnasium at the high school to a 5,700-seat sports arena on the campus of the University of Akron to sell more tickets. The cost for parents to see their sons participate in sports increased from $3 or $4 per game to $12 to $15 per game (Associated Press, 2003).

In addition, many of his away games were played in ten-thousand-plus seat arenas around the country, of which many of the schools paid his high school as much as $10,000 per contest. All of his team's home games were broadcast on pay-per-view television at a cost of $8 per game. Cable sports giant ESPN broadcasted one of his high school games, the first nationally televised high school sporting event ever (Donegan, 2003).

Moreover, the competitive nature and the zero-sum outcome structure of athletic performances place greater evaluative weight on individual successes and failures, outcomes that are immediately visible to an interested public. This sort of performance pressure, a defining characteristic of the athlete role, is rarely encountered in other social role enactments in schools (e.g., the chemistry test).

Eventually, a performance-based public athletic reputation is forged in which the athlete comes to realize that his or her athlete identity is joined to a larger community (team, school, hometown, state, and country). The athlete further realizes that the collective esteem of this larger community can rise and fall as a result of his or her athletic performance (Derpinghaus, 2001). The public reputation of most successful athletes is generally positive, carrying a high degree of social status and esteem. Psychologically fortified by this public acclaim, the athlete's public athletic reputation becomes part of his or her overall identity.

Balancing the Academic Role

As alluded to earlier, the academic role and the athletic role of a student-athlete are often in conflict and misunderstood. The perception by many in the school setting is that athletes take easier classes because they are "dumb jocks" and do not care much about academics (Sailes, 1993). Others assume athletes receive special treatment from teachers (Bowen & Levin, 2003). Upon closer scrutiny, one realizes that many athletes work as hard in the classroom as they do on the field. One also realizes that athletes lead more hectic lives than normal students because of their athletic identity. They are expected to be students, athletes, public figures, and role models, all at the same time. They start the day at the same time as all other students and attend classes for the same length of time. When the bell rings, sounding the end of the day for average students, the student-athlete begins his or her extracurricular activity day. They put in long, hard hours of practice that often exceed the number of restricted hours allotted by sports governing bodies.

These long and laborious hours often infringe on time other students use for studying (Kellogg, 2001). Increasingly, voluntary practices are no longer "voluntary," even during the off-season.

According to sociologist Harry Edwards (as cited in Stoll & Beller, 1998), student-athletes are programmed to fail. Because they have forsaken other roles in pursuit of the athletic role, Edwards contends that many student-athletes are academically unprepared. He also asserts that because they spend so much time practicing and playing sports, they are perpetually fatigued; all of which, he says, is a blueprint for educational mediocrity and failure (Stoll & Beller, 1998).

Gender Role Identity and Sports

All student-athletes are not recognized the same within the public space of schools. Indeed, males and females are recognized quite differently. This difference can be attributed, in large part, to what society views as the appropriate role for boys and girls. Our society has expectations about appropriate behaviors, attitudes, beliefs, and values for males and females. From a very early age, boys and girls are socialized differently and taught different gender roles. Boys are expected to act masculine while women are expected to act feminine (Bartky, 1990). Sports are a masculine domain and engaging in sporting activities is considered masculine behavior (Lenskyj, 1990).

Although many institutions in society perform this socialization process, a great part of it occurs in schools. In schools, certain sports are acceptable for boys and certain sports are acceptable for girls. For example, football is considered acceptable for boys, while field hockey is acceptable for girls. Baseball is acceptable for boys while softball is acceptable for girls. Students who cross the boundaries are viewed as abnormal or different (Blinde & Taub, 1992).

This difference in recognition based on gender has limited the opportunities for girls to participate in some sports and for women to coach or direct sports programs. According to Lumpkin, Stoll, and Beller (2003), "Societal expectations about appropriate feminine behavior and gender-bound roles curtailed women's active participation in sports until relatively recent times" (183). Sex-role stereotyping has a profound impact on female participation in, and attitudes toward, sports. Girls are less likely than boys to be given adequate coaching in sports, to be exposed to a wide variety of sports experiences in their youth, or to have highly visible role models (Lumpkin, Stoll, & Beller, 2003).

In families and schools, boys and girls are rewarded for gender behavior that is considered appropriate, and discouraged for behavior that is not considered appropriate. Girls are generally taught and expected to be emotional, maternal, compassionate, gentle, nonassertive, and dependent—all of which are believed to be counterproductive to success in sport. Boys, on the other hand, are expected to be strong, competitive, assertive, confident, aggressive, and independent—all traits believed necessary to be successful in sport (Bartky, 1990).

Boys who are successful in sports receive a great deal of praise and attention from the media. Girls receive much less attention and coverage and fewer accolades. According to Tuggle (1997) the media gives most of its coverage to male athletes while largely ignoring female athletes. When girls are accorded status and peer recognition, it is generally based on their good looks and attractive clothes (i.e., they look very feminine). They are not taken as seriously as boys, and they are seen as objects to be looked at, sexualized, made fun of, or trivialized (Young, 1997).

The bodies of boys and girls change dramatically during the school-age years, as does the increased understanding and importance of interpersonal relationships. During these years, students' self-focus and awareness of their peers evaluations of them are heightened (Lapsley, Milstead, Quintana, Flannery, & Buss, 1986). Body image plays a major role in students' self-esteem (Abell & Richards, 1996; Polce-Lynch, Myers, Kilmartin, Forssmann-Falck, & Kliewer, 1998). Both female and male students place more importance on their appearance than adults, and report higher levels of body dissatisfaction (Cash, Winstead, & Janda, 1986). These findings clearly imply that appearance is a highly significant aspect of students' identity.

Because they train and practice so much, athletes tend to have leaner and more muscular bodies than nonathletes. Even though having a lean, muscular body is considered positive and desirable, there are still limits as to how much athletic ability, strength, and muscularity are socially acceptable for girls. The expectations of female body image is to be toned and not too muscular. Excessive musculature on a girl is considered masculine and socially unacceptable. It also provides the impetus for the athlete to be labeled as lesbian by her peers. While being fit is increasingly valued for females, it is still important to "look nice." Bordo (1993) elaborates on the paradox of muscle development for women:

> A tight, toned body is perceived as ideal, yet large muscles symbolize strength and masculinity and are not feminine. Therefore female athletes often struggle with the contradiction of the desire to be strong and toned while not developing "oversized" musculature. (211)

While girls struggle with their athletic identity and, particularly, labeling, boys learn to be proud of having strong and powerful bodies.

Schools and Sports

When we talk about student success in schools and athletics, the conversation is packed with references that instantly bring forth common American values. We seem to scarcely notice the baggage that the pursuit of these values has in shaping the identity of our students.

As students navigate through a world of ESPN highlights, McDonald's arches, Nike swooshes, and Gatorade drinks, their view of the role of schooling can easily be altered. Students are an easy mark for the myriad of advertisements, commercials, and corporate regalia. The mass media counts on this power of influence to transmit its own set of values to school-aged students. Sports images in popular culture are lavish with promises of success for students. Every day, television advertisements, posters, magazines, and clothing convey familiar images: idealized body types, school-aged athletes foregoing college to play professional sports to make millions of dollars, and successful athletes sporting the "bling."

Although there are far more successful teachers, doctors, and lawyers than there are successful professional athletes, students would never know it from the images that surround them daily.

Not surprisingly, student identity is influenced by these images, but in the wrong direction. Instead of being influenced in the direction of the value of a good education, they are being led to devalue the educational experience in pursuit of the athletic experience.

Now, more than ever, these two identities are in conflict. But as difficult and stressful as these role conflicts may be, they do contribute to the process of identity formation and constitute the normal and predictable growth stages experienced by students as they strive to develop an identity.

In assisting students in coping with these identity challenges, schools must first give the issue serious attention. Schools are the only institutions charged with extending the values of home and family into communities and society; they are the medium for transmitting ideals. Schools must be aware of the potential tension between the need for peer approval and a sense of belonging, the time commitments needed for sports and study, and the ongoing stresses students experience as they strive to develop a personal identity. It is also important for schools to recognize that as stressful as role conflicts may be, they are a normal part of growth that students must resolve in making a successful transition to adulthood.

Schools must work with athletes, coaches, and parents to clearly state their belief in the intellectual potential of student-athletes and to make explicit the purpose, mission, and value of schooling and the role of athletics. Athletics should be recognized as secondary to the school's mission of educating boys and girls to become productive members of society—tomorrow's leaders.

Schools must emphasize, recognize, and creatively reward participation and academic scholarship in the classroom for the many, not just sporting accomplishments and college scholarships for the most athletically talented few. They must help students understand that opportunities to play organized athletics beyond high school are available to only a select few and that the stories of people like Lebron James are one in a million. Educators who understand this offer the truest hope in getting students and society to understand that chemistry is truly more important than football.

References

Abell, S., & Richards, M. (1996). The relationship between body shape satisfaction and self-esteem: An investigation of gender and class differences. *Journal of Youth and Adolescence, 25*(5), 691–703.

Associated Press. (2003, January 13). *With James driving like a pro, eligibility questioned.* Retrieved March 17, 2004, from espn.go.com/nba/news/2003/0112/1491511.html

Bartky, S. (1990). *Femininity and domination: Studies in the phenomenology of oppression.* New York: Routledge.

Bennett, W. (1998). A nation still at risk. *Policy Review, 90*(4), 23–30.

Bingham, C. (2001). *Schools of recognition: Identity politics and classroom practices.* Lanham, MD: Rowman & Littlefield Publishers.

Blinde, E., & Taub, D. (1992). Women athletes as falsely accused deviants: Managing the lesbian stigma. *Sociological Quarterly, 33*(4), 521–33.

Bordo, S. (1993). *Unbearable weight: Feminism, western culture, and the body.* Berkeley: University of California Press.

Bowen, W., & Levin, S. (2003). *Reclaiming the game: College sports and educational values.* Princeton, NJ: Princeton University Press.

Brewer, B., Van Raalte, J., & Linder, D. (1993). Athletic identity: Hercules' muscles or Achilles' heel? *International Journal of Sport Psychology, 24*(2), 237–54.

Cash, T., Winstead, B., & Janda, L. (1986). The great American shape-up: Body image survey report. *Psychology Today, 20*(4), 30–37.

Chickering, A., & Reisser, L. (1993). *Education and identity* (Second Ed.). San Francisco: Jossey-Bass.

Cornelius, A. (1995). The relationship between athletic identity, peer and faculty socialization, and college student development. *Journal of College Student Development, 36*(6), 560–73.

Derpinghaus, T. (2001). Handling the mass media's hype. Retrieved December 15, 2001, from www.dailycardinal.com

Donegan, L. (2003). *America's most wanted.* Retrieved July 7, 2003, from observer.guardian.co.uk/osm/story/0,6903,904352,00.html

Edwards, H. (2000). Crisis of black athletes on the eve of the 21st century. *Society, 37*(3), 9–13.

Goldberg, A. (1991). Counseling the high school student-athlete. *School Counselor, 38*(5), 332–40.

Goldberg, A., & Chandler, T. (1989). The role of athletics in the social world of high school students. *Youth and Society, 21*(2), 238–50.

Guttman, A. (1991). The anomaly of intercollegiate athletics. In J. Andre & D. James (Eds.), *Rethinking college athletics* (17–30). Philadelphia: Temple University Press.

Kane, M. (1988). The female athletic role as a status determinant within the social systems of high school adolescents. *Adolescence, 23*(90), 253–64.

Kellogg, A. (2001). For athletes, how much practice time is too much? *Chronicle of Higher Education, 47*(38), A33–A34.

Lapchick, R. (1987–1988). The high school athlete as the future college student-athlete. *Journal of Sport and Social Issues, 11*(1-2), 104–24.

Lapsley, D., Milstead, M., Quintana, S., Flannery, D., & Buss, R. (1986). Adolescent egocentrism and formal operations: Tests of a theoretical assumption. *Developmental Psychology, 22*(6), 800–807.

Lauer, H. (2002). *Sports participation: The metaphor of youth development.* Retrieved May 15, 2002, from www.americansportsdata.com/

Lenskyj, H. (1990). Power and play: Gender and sexuality issues in sport and physical activity. *International Review for Sociology of Sport, 25*(3), 235–45.

Lumpkin, A., Stoll, S., & Beller, J. (2003). *Sport ethics: Applications for fair play.* New York: McGraw-Hill.

Messerli, J. (1972). *Horace Mann: A biography.* New York: Random House.

Polce-Lynch, M., Myers, B., Kilmartin, C., Forssmann-Falck, R., & Kliewer, W. (1998). Gender and age patterns in emotional expression, body image, and self-esteem: A qualitative analysis. *Sex Roles, 38*(11-12), 1025–48.

Ryska, T. (2002). The effects of athletic identity and motivation goals on global competence perceptions of student-athletes. *Child Study Journal, 32*(2), 109–29.

Sailes, G. (1993). An investigation of campus stereotypes: The myth of black athletic superiority and the dumb jock stereotype. *Sociology of Sports Journal, 10*(1), 88–97.

Snyder, E. (1985). A theoretical analysis of academic and athletic roles. *Sociology of Sport Journal, 2*(3), 211–17.

Stoll, S., & Beller, J. (1998). *SBH ethical standard: A unique teaching methodology for moral reasoning.* Moscow, ID: Author.

Taylor, E. (1999). Bring in "da noise": Race, sports, and the role of schools. *Educational Leadership, 56*(7), 75–78.

Thirer, J., & Wright, S. (1985). Sport and social status for adolescent males and females. *Sociology of Sport Journal, 2*(2), 164–71.

Tuggle, C. (1997). Differences in television sports reporting of men's and women's athletics: ESPN Sportscenter and CNN Sports Tonight. *Journal of Broadcasting and Electronic Media, 41*(1), 14–24.

U.S. Department of Education. (2001). *Ages for compulsory school attendance, special education services for students, policies for year-round schools and kindergarten programs by state: 1997–2000.* Washington, DC: U.S. Department of Education.

Williams, J., & White, K. (1983). Adolescent status system for males and females at three age levels. *Adolescence, 18*(70), 381–89.

Williams, M., & Anderson, M. (1987). Influence of sex and gender roles on high school status systems. *Adolescence, 22*(88), 755–65.

Young, K. (1997). Women, sport, & physicality. *International Review for the Sociology of Sport, 32*(3), 297–305.

10

Parental Involvement: Low Socioeconomic Status (SES) and Ethnic Minority Parents' Struggle for Recognition and Identity

Julia Ballenger

Research has shown that increased involvement on the part of parents in schools positively affects cognitive and social functioning of children (Henderson & Mapp, 2002). Similarly, in Notes from Research, it was found that students with involved parents were more likely to "(1) earn higher grades and tests scores, (2) be promoted, (3) attend school regularly, and (4) graduate and go on to postsecondary education" (para. 1, 1997). Therefore, expanding the involvement of low SES and ethnic minority parents in the education of their children would appear to be an important strategy to advance the effectiveness of and improve the quality of education (Espstein, 1995; Chrispeels, 1996; Scheerens & Bosker, 1997).

The central purpose of this chapter is to discuss the involvement of low SES and ethnic minority parents in their children's education from the perspective of the politics of recognition and identity formation. The context of this chapter addresses (1) changing demographics, (2) achievement gaps between ethnic minority groups and white students, (3) the principal's role in parental involvement, (4) barriers to low SES and ethnic minority parental involvement, (5) overcoming barriers to low SES and ethnic minority parental involvement through the politics of recognition and identity formation, and (6) conclusions.

Changing Demographics

The U.S. Census Bureau uses a set of money-income thresholds that vary by family size and composition. A family is considered poor or low SES, along with each individual in it, if the family's total income is less than that family's threshold. Therefore, low SES parents are defined as parents whose total income is less than the family's threshold (National Center for Education Statistics, 2002). The term "ethnic minority" refers to people of color, specifically African American and Hispanic parents.

The racial and ethnic composition of public school students in kindergarten through twelfth grade between 1972 and 2004 has increased. 43 percent of public school students were considered to be part of a racial or ethnic minority group in 2004, an increase from 22 percent in 1972. In comparison, the percentage of public school students who were white decreased from 78 to 57 percent. The minority increase was largely due to growth in the proportion of students who were Hispanic. In 2004, Hispanic students represented 19 percent of public school enrollment, up from 6 percent in 1972.

The proportion of public school students who were black or who were members of other minority groups increased less over this period than the proportion of students who were Hispanic: black students made up 16 percent of public school enrollment in 2004, compared with 15 percent in 1972. Hispanic enrollment surpassed black enrollment for the first time in 2002 (National Center for Education Statistics, 2004a). While reform efforts have been instrumental in lessening the achievement gap between white students and students of color, the achievement gap continues to exist.

Achievement Gap

According to the "2004 Trends in Average Reading Scale Scores by Race/Ethnicity: White-Black Gap," key findings revealed that black students average reading scores in 2004 were higher than in 1971. For nine-year-olds, both white and black students scored higher in 2004 than in any previous assessment year. The white-black gap decreased between 1971 (forty-four points) and 2004 (twenty-six points) (National Center for Education Statistics, 2004b).

In regard to thirteen-year-olds, the average scores of both white and black students were significantly higher in 2004 than in 1971. The white-black gap in 2004 (twenty-two points) was smaller than in 1971 (thirty-nine points). Seventeen-year-old black students' average score was higher in 2004 than in 1971, while white students' scores in 1971 and 2004 were not statistically different. While the achievement gap is too wide, on a positive note, the gap between white and black students was smaller in 2004 (twenty-nine points) than in 1971 (fifty-three points) (National Center for Education Statistics, 2004b).

Likewise, in the 2004 "Trends in Average Reading Scale Scores by Race/Ethnicity: White-Hispanic Gap," key findings revealed that Hispanic students' average reading scale scores were higher in 2004 than in 1975. For nine-year-olds, white and Hispanic students' average scale scores were higher in 2004 than in 1975 and 1999. The white-Hispanic reading score gap in 2004 (twenty-one points) was significantly smaller than it was in 1975 (thirty-four points). In regards to thirteen-year-olds, the average scale scores of white and Hispanic students were higher in 2004 than in 1975. There was no statistically significant difference between white-Hispanic gaps in 2004 and 1975. For seventeen-year-olds, Hispanic students scored higher in 2004 than in 1975, while white students' average score in 2004 was not statistically different from that in 1975. The score gap between white and Hispanic students was smaller in 2004 (twenty-nine points) than in 1975 (forty-one points). (National Center for Education Statistics, 2004b).

The Principal's Role in Parental Involvement

When parents are involved with their children and involved with the school, their children experience greater academic success. This situation is true from the preschool years through high school. This acknowledgement of the importance of parent involvement is built on research findings accumulated over two decades that show children have an advantage in school when their parents are interested in and support their school activities (Coleman et al., 1966; Clausen, 1966; McDill & Ribsby, 1973; Lightfoot, 1978; Epstein & McPartland, 1979).

Epstein (1983) suggests, "It is the principal's role to orchestrate activities that will help the staff study and understand parent involvement, and to select or design, evaluate, and revise programs for parental involvement" (121). Thus, it is critical that principals create networks between parents and educators in order to develop a school culture that is more inviting for low SES and ethnic minority parents. The principal may increase parent involvement with their children's education and school by demonstrating the following practices.

- Demonstrate to parents and educators that when they are actively involved in their children's education, the result is improved grades, test scores, attendance, etc.
- Encourage teachers to develop an effective attitude toward parental involvement.
- Recognize and move past the roadblocks that have stood in the way of parent and teacher communication. (National African American Parent Day Involvement, n.d.)

To improve the education of low SES and marginalized families, principals and staff must foster positive school attitudes toward low SES and marginalized families and empower these parents to become involved in the school. Parents should be encouraged to participate in meaningful roles and given an opportunity to provide substantive, specific, and positive feedback (Comer & Haynes, 1991). Furthermore, "the principal's role in creating a welcoming school climate is especially important because sustainable improvements in school, family, and community relationships require continuous, active, and well-informed leadership that emphasizes meeting parent, teacher, and student needs over time" (Hoover-Dempsey, Walker, Sandler, Whetsel, Green, Wilkins, & Closson, 2005, 155).

The research confirms that parental involvement is not an option in high-poverty schools; it is a requirement of various federal programs—for good reasons. The 2001 No Child Left Behind Act (NCLB) recognizes that families are an asset to student achievement and help students become engaged in their schooling. NCLB is designed to help close the achievement gap between disadvantaged and minority students and their peers. Additionally, measures were put into place to change the culture of America's schools so that success is defined in terms of student achievement and the school's interest in every child's success (U.S. Department of Education, 2002).

Griffith (2001) as cited in Hoover-Dempsey and colleagues (2005) found that "school administrators set the tone for parental involvement and program implementation" (117). Thus, the principal should be aware of what constitutes parental involvement under NCLB and should encourage low SES and ethnic minority parents to (1) play an integral role in assisting their child's learning, (2) to be actively involved in their child's education, and that (3) to become full partners in their child's education and (4) to include, as appropriate, these parents on advisory committees to assist in the education of their child.

The principal should also act within policy and guidelines of the parental involvement requirements in NCLB, which specifically establishes the local campus' expectations for parental involvement. The loss of Title I, Part A funding may occur if campuses do not implement programs, activities, and procedures for the involvement of parents in Title I, Part A programs consistent with Section 1118 (U.S. Department of Education, 2004).

Barriers to Low-SES and Ethnic Minority Parental Involvement

Some school staff may perceive limited involvement of these parents in school as a lack of interest in their children's education; however, strong support in literature shows low SES parents care about their children's education and are providing support for their children (Moles, 1993; Swap, 1993; Terrell, 2002; Mapp, 2002).

For these parents, education is way out of poverty. However, Moles found that several factors prevail that may account for lower rates of contact and collaboration. The first factor is limited skills and knowledge among parents on which to build collaboration. Herein, literacy and lack of fluency in English impedes parents' ability to interact with the school. In general, the educational jargon and complex verbal construction further impede communication for disadvantaged parents.

Another factor is restricted opportunities for interaction. In many low SES families, both parents work outside the home and have difficulty attending conferences during the school day. Cultural differences in values, goals, purpose of education, and an understanding of appropriate roles of parents and schools serve as other factors that inhibit parent involvement (Delgado-Gaitan 1991). Still other obstacles such as misperceptions, negative expectations, and distrust may also serve as barriers. Thus, many low SES parents may not feel comfortable in schools.

According to Hoover-Dempsey and Sandler's (1997) body of research, low SES parents' belief about what is necessary, important, and permissible for parents to do is different from that of upper-middle-class parents. Working-class parents view their role in their children's school as limited. On the other hand, upper-middle-class parents believe their role is critical in their children receiving access to a quality education. The parents' sense of efficacy may be another barrier. Parents who believe they can help their children academically, even those whose education level is not high, will be more active in the school. Finally, parents' perception of the school as inviting or uninviting will determine their level of participation. Parents are sensitive to negative signs and are wary of unauthentic invitations to participate.

Three decades ago Lightfoot (1978) recognized that racism in schools such as paternalism and lowered expectations for minority students tend to act as barriers to parent contact and collaboration. More recently, Crozier's (2001) study recognized deracialization in parent involvement policies as a barrier. Policies that fail to address race and ethnicity issues as related to parental involvement may contribute to the marginalization and discrimination of ethnic minority parents. The "one-size fits" all model of parental involvement assumes that all parents are the same. Even ethnic minority and low SES parents are not alike and are intersected by class, gender, age, physical ability, sexuality, and experiences that may affect their expressions of ethnic identity.

While attention to academic achievement gaps between ethnic minority and white students are addressed in some parental involvement policies and research, no references are made to racial inequalities and antiracist education. This lack of recognition often results in schools' unawareness of the need to address issues of structural racism and possible marginalization of some low SES and ethnic minority parents. It should be noted in the NCLB addresses only parents whose primary language is not English, migratory parents, and parents of students with disabilities. All other strategies for parental involvement imply that all parents are the same.

Differences between the vision and values of the dominant culture and that of ethnic minority cultures may also serve as a barrier to parental involvement. Crozier (2001) states,

> Schools function, it is argued, on the basis of harmonious and unified vision and values. Parent participation thus poses a potential threat to this, in particular where the parent body holds diverse vision and values; the threat may be heightened when ethnic minority parents are involved, given the expectation or perception that their value position will be different from the dominant positions. (332)

Active participation and representation are central to participatory democracy. White middle-class parents have the social capital and resources to make their voices heard in school. Thus, schools that claim they want low SES and ethnic minority parents to be involved in their children's school and education must be aware of the need to empower these parents, provide equal opportunity to participate, and allow their voices to be heard. On the other hand, ignoring their voices is a form of marginalization. This form of marginalization renders low SES and ethnic minority parents invisible (Crozier, 2000).

Overcoming Barriers to Low SES and Ethnic Minority Parent Involvement

I suggest that viewing barriers to low SES and ethnic minority parent involvement through the lens of "recognition" may provide principals with a conceptual framework in which to develop strategies to eliminate these barriers. The concept of recognition is not new. This concept starts from the Hegelian idea that identity is constructed dialogically, through mutual recognition. Hegel in *The Phenomenology of the Spirit* conceptualized recognition as a distinctive need of human beings (Chandhoke, 1999).

Fraser (2000) notes that the "recognition" or "identity mode" transposes the Hegelian recognition schema onto cultural and political terrain and refers to it as "the politics of recognition" or the "identity model." He continues, "One becomes an individual subject only by virtue of recognizing, and being recognized by, another subject. Recognition from others is thus essential to the development of a sense of self. To be denied recognition—or to be 'misrecognized'—is to suffer both a distortion of one's relation to one's self and an injury to one's identity" (2).

The proponents of politics of recognition contend that to belong to a group that is devalued by the dominant culture is to be misrecognized. As a result of repeated encounters with the stigmatizing gaze of a culturally dominant other, members internalize negative self images. Furthermore, Fraser posits that "the politics of recognition aims [sic] to repair this negative image by proposing that members of misrecognized groups reject such images in favor self-representations of their own making—which, publicly asserted, will gain the respect and esteem of society at large. The results, when successful, results in 'recognition': an undistorted relation to oneself" (2000, 2).

Additionally, Charles Taylor (1994) and Axel Honneth (1998) framed their political theory on the concept of recognition. Taylor defines recognition as "notice or attention accorded to a thing or person." Furthermore, he stated, "Recognition has to do with affirming another person" (57).

Taylor (1994) argues that "due recognition is not just a courtesy we owe people, it is a vital human need" (60). Chandhoke (1999) states that recognition at its basic level "indicates that we become conscious of ourselves when we see that others have become conscious of us; however, at a deeper level, recognition indicates that people need approval and respect of others in order to develop self-esteem, self-confidence and self-respect" (4). Many times low SES and ethnic minority parents are treated as outsiders in their children's school. Principals and teachers must show mutual respect for all parents.

Rather than treating parents as disconnected individuals, administrators should work with school staff to create an understanding of diverse cultures, languages, and ethnicity. Administrators need to develop a school culture of inclusiveness rather than exclusiveness. Identity recognition focuses on the needs of both insider and outsider recognition. Low-SES and ethnic minority parents need recognition as people who matter and who matter equally.

Fraser (2000) in Rethinking Recognition contends that recognition should be understood as a question of social status rather than existential address. From this perspective, Fraser stated, "What requires recognition is not group-specific identity but the status of individual group members as full partners in social interaction" (4). Thus, misrecognition refers to social subordination. Fraser continues by stating,

> To address this injustice still requires a politic of recognition, but in the "status model" this means a politics aimed at overcoming insubordination by establishing the misrecognized part as a full member of society, capable of participating on par with the rest of us. (4)

Low-SES and ethnic minority parents must be recognized as capable participants in their children's school and education. Principals should strive to eliminate misrecognition and status subordination by studying patterns of cultural value on the campus and becoming aware of teacher's attitudes, beliefs, and values that consider some parents as deficient or inferior. Fraser (2000) posits that the goal in redressing misrecognition is to replace value patterns that "impede parity of participation with ones that enable or foster it" (5).

All parents should be invited to fully participate in their child's education and school. Lopez, Scribner, and Mahitivanichcha (2001) state that "efforts to increase parent involvement should not be based on the assumption that parents who are not involved lack the capacity to provide adequate home learning environments for their children or that they are not involved in their children's schooling at home" (215, as cited in Lee & Bowen, 2006). This misrecognition of parents as fully capable partners results in deficit thinking. Valencia (1997) posited, "Deficit thinking not only devalues the educational involvement exhibited by parents from nondominant groups, but also takes attention away from the professional responsibility of schools to establish effective parent involvement programs for those families" (215, as cited in Lee & Bowen, 2006).

The beliefs, attitudes, and values of parents and teachers differ and are culturally determined. This is particularly true of low SES and ethnic minority parents. School, for such parents, often constitutes a foreign place, a place where they do not feel at home or a place where they think they do not belong, keeping these parents on the sidelines (Driessen & Valkenberg, 2000; Vincent & Martin, 2002). Constant dialogue among the principal, school staff, and low SES and ethnic minority parents is essential. When low SES and ethnic minority parents are accepted as equal partners in the education of their children, it becomes a win-win situation for all.

Conclusion

In some schools children of color and low SES have not been well served in the past. The achievement gap among children of color and white children is certainly too wide. Perceptions among the uninformed public that parents who are members of low SES and ethnic minority groups are not interested in their children's education is inaccurate. Equally damaging is the false belief that education is not valued by these families and communities. We as a society share in the responsibility of educating all children.

Thirty years ago Lightfoot (1978) wrote, "In an effort to initiate and sustain productive interactions with parents, educators must begin by searching for strength (not pathology) in children and their families" (42). Low SES and ethnic minority parents need to be affirmed, not merely tolerated. They need to be empowered to participate meaningfully in their children's school and education. The principal sets the tone for guiding teachers and staff in developing a warm and inviting climate for all parents.

References

Chandhoke, N. (1999). The logic of recognition. Retrieved May 17, 2004, from www.india-seminar.com/1999/484/484%20chandhoke.htm

Chrispeels, J. (1996). Effective schools and home-school-community partnership roles: A framework for parent involvement. *School Effectiveness and School Improvement, 7*(4), 297–324.

Clausen, J. A. (1966). Family structure, socialization and personality. In L. W. Hoffman and M. L. Hoffman (Eds.), *Review of child development research*, Vol. 2. (1–53). New York: Russell Sage.

Coleman, J. S., Campbell, E. Q., Hobson, C. J., McPartland, J. M., Mood, A., Weinfield, F. D., & York, R. L. (1966). *Equal educational opportunity*. Washington, DC: Government Printing Office.

Comer, J. P., & Haynes, N. M. (1991). Parent involvement in schools: An ecological approach. *Elementary School Journal, 91*(3), 271–77.

Crozier, G. (2000). *Parents and schools: Partners or protagonists?* Stoke-on-Trent: Trentham Books.

Crozier, G. (2001). Excluded parents: The deracialisation of parental involvement. *Race Ethnicity and Education, 4*(4), 330–41.

Delgado-Gaitan, C. (1991). Involving parents in the schools: A process of empowerment. *American Journal of Education, 100*(1), 20–46.

Driessen, G., & Valkenberg, P. (2000). Islamic schools in the Netherlands: Compromising between identity and quality? *British Journal of Religious Education, 23*(1), 15–26.

Epstein, J. L. (1983). Longitudinal effects of person-family-school interactions on student outcomes. In A. Kerchhoff (Ed.), *Research in sociology of education and socialization*, Vol. 4 (119–30). Greenwich, CN: Jai

Epstein, J. L. (1995). *School/family/community partnerships: Preparing educators and improving schools*. Boulder, CO: Westview.

Epstein, J. L., & McPartland, J. M. (1979). Authority structures. In H. Walberg (Ed.), *Educational Environments and Effects* (293–310). Berkeley, CA: McCutcheon.

Fraser, N. (2000, May–June). Rethinking recognition. New Left Review. Retrieved August 12, 2004, from newleftreview.org/A2248

Griffith, J. (2001). Principal leadership of parent involvement. *Journal of Educational Administration, 39*(2), 162–86.

Henderson, A., & Mapp, K. (2002). A new wave of evidence: The impact of school, family, community connections on student achievement. Annual synthesis. Austin, TX, Southwest Education Development Laboratory.

Honneth, A. (1998). *The struggle for recognition: The moral grammar of social conflicts.* Cambridge: Polity Press.

Hoover-Dempsey, K. V., & Sandler, H. M. (1997, Spring). Why do parents become involved in their children's education? *Review of Educational Research, 67*(1), 3–42.

Hoover-Dempsey, K. V., Walker, J. M. T., Sandler, H. M., Whetsel, D., Green, C. L, Wilkins, A. S., & Closson, K. (2005). Why do parents become involved? Research findings and implications. *Elementary School Journal, 106*(2), 105–30.

Lee, J. S., & Bowen, N. K. (2006). Parent involvement, cultural capital, and the achievement gap among elementary school children. *American Educational Research Journal, 43*(2), 193–218.

Lightfoot, S. L. (1978). *Worlds apart.* New York: Basic Books.

Lopez, G., Scribner, J., & Mahitivanichcha, K. (2001). Redefining parental involvement: Lessons from high-performing migrant-impacted schools. *American Educational Research Journal, 38*(2), 253–88.

Mapp, K. L. (2002). Having their say: Parents describe how and why they are involved in their children's education. Paper presented at the Annual Meeting of the American Educational Research Association, New Orleans, LA.

McDill, E. L., & Rigsby, L. R. (1973). *Structure and process in secondary schools: The academic impact of educational climates.* Baltimore: Johns Hopkins University Press.

Moles, O. C. (1993). Collaboration between schools and disadvantaged parents: Obstacles and openings. In N. F. Chavkin (Ed.), *Families and schools in a pluralistic society.* Albany: State University of New York Press.

National African American Parent Involvement Day (n.d.) Planning national African American parent involvement day. Retrieved August 15, 2004, from www.naapid.org/N-planning.html

National Center for Education Statistics (2002). The condition of education 2002. Retrieved May 17, 2004, from nces.ed.gov/Pubsearch/pubsinfo.asp?pubid =2002025

National Center for Education Statistics (2004a). The percentage of racial/ethnic minority students enrolled in the nation's public schools increased between 1972 and 2004, primarily due to growth in Hispanic enrollments. Retrieved May 17, 2005, from nces.ed.gov/programs/coe/2006/section1/indicator05.asp

National Center for Education Statistics (2004b). Trends in Average Reading Scale Scores by Race/Ethnicity: White-Black Gap. Retrieved May 17, 2005, from nces.ed.gov/nationsreportcard/ltt/results2004/sub-reading-race.asp

No Child Left Behind. Public Law 107–110. (2005, July). Guidance for the implementation of Title I, Part A, improving basic programs operated by local education agencies. Division of NCLB Program Coordination, Texas Education Agency.

Scheerens, J., & Bosker, R. (1997). *The foundations of educational effectiveness.* Oxford: Elsevier Science.

Swap, S. M. (1993). *Developing home-school partnerships: From concepts to practice.* New York: Teachers College Press.

Taylor, C. (1994). *Multiculturalism: Examining the politics of recognition.* Princeton, NJ: Princeton University Press.

Terrell, S. R. (2002). Parents speak about parent involvement. Paper presented at the Annual Meeting of the American Educational Research Association. New Orleans, LA.

Valencia, R. R. (1997). Conceptualizing the notion of deficit thinking. In R. R. Valencia (Ed.), *The evolution of deficit thinking: Educational thought and practice* (1–12). Bristol, PA: Falmer.

Vincent, C., & Martin, J. (2002). Class, culture, and agency: Researching parental voice. *Discourse, 23*(1), 109–28.

U.S. Department of Education. (2002, April). Testing for results: Helping families, schools, and communities understand and improve student achievement. Retrieved May 19, 2004, from www.ed.gov/index.jhtml

U.S. Department of Education. (2004, April). Parental involvement: Title I Part A. Retrieved May 19, 2004, from www.ed.gov/programs/titleiparta/parentinvguid .doc

11

Reaching Out to Parents as Partners in Preparing Students for Postsecondary Education

Betty Alford

Diverse student needs call for personalized academic advocacy and social and emotional support from parents as well as the school in order to impact students' success in preparing for college admission and retention (Tierney, 2006). Student success is fostered when the community and parents become committed partners in the educational process (Scribner & Reyes, 1999). Parents can participate meaningfully in their children's preparation for success in postsecondary education when they are given knowledge about recommended secondary courses for college preparation as well as the availability of financial aid (Tierney, 2006). However, parents of low socioeconomic groups may lack the knowledge of ways to assist their children in navigating secondary school courses and processes in preparation for postsecondary education (Noguera, 2003).

Olivérez (2006) describes the difficulty that many first-generation college-goers face:

> Many low income, first-generation college-goers have parents who support their educational endeavors but possess little understanding of what it takes for their child to get admitted to college. These parents, most of whom are immigrants, want nothing

more than for their child to succeed academically and have a better quality of life, but many are unclear as to how to help make this happen. In a neighborhood where most residents work multiple jobs to make ends meet, survival is often their first priority. (74)

Tierney (2006), in his study of low-income students' experiences in Esperanza High School, a large high school in the Los Angeles United School District, further emphasized, "The challenge for these students was to find, or more likely create, a web of social and academic networks that helped them plan for college" (137). Noguera's (2003) study of Berkeley High School also observed that low socioeconomic parents were less likely to question the rigor of students' academic work or the course sequence students were taking compared to middle and high socioeconomic parents. They were less likely than middle and high economic parents to engage in informal networks of conversation with other parents about college preparatory activities.

Students also may not question courses needed for postsecondary education. Olivérez (2006) reported, from his work in Esperanza High School, that counselors track students instead of registering students for courses designed to meet their career goals: "The average Esperanza student takes the courses their overburdened 'track counselors' program them into failing to question whether or not these courses will help prepare them to meet their purported goals" (76).

Tierney's (2006) observations and interviews at Esperanza High School led him to conclude that college information was rarely received by minority, low-income parents and students before it was too late to meet college admission deadlines. Tierney emphasized the need to share college information with parents by stating,

> Many parents are able to play a role (in helping their children get to college) and they will benefit from systematic, structured information. Too often, these parents were not equipped with information in a timely manner. Thus, they were able to lend their moral and emotional support to their children, but they could have done more to assist in preparing for college if they had been provided the necessary information and skills. (141)

Tierney further suggested, "It might be useful to think of college as a foreign land, first-generation students and their parents as potential tourists, and those of us in the educational system as travel agents" (142).

Although there is often a decline in parental involvement with schools when students are in high school, school outreach efforts can reverse this decline (Eccles & Harold, 1993). Plank and Jordon (1997) reported that increased communication between parents, high school students, and school personnel about postsecondary education and academic matters increased students' chances of enrolling in postsecondary education. In a study of ten high schools with a diverse student population, parents were identified as most influential in students' decisions to take Advanced Placement (AP) courses (Ndura, Robinson, & Ochs, 2003). Parents can also serve as active partners in making schools more socially just by challenging prevailing beliefs that limit student's academic growth (Oakes, Rogers, & Lipton, 2006).

However, challenges in connecting with parents may arise (Tierney, 2006). Tierney reported concerning recent immigrants, "Connecting with parents, many of whom are struggling to find work and raise children in a new and strange country, is a constant challenge for teachers and school leaders" (54). Pena (2000) found that limited English-speaking parents thought their attendance at meetings conducted only in English were unnecessary because of the language barrier. Pena stressed, "Information must be available in the parent's native language and teachers need to use social networks to keep parents informed" (52). There is a need to engage in practices and processes to promote parents as partners in preparing students for postsecondary education (Olivérez, 2006).

This chapter will provide a discussion of the importance of course-taking patterns to students' success in postsecondary education and the benefits of advanced level courses to students' academic growth. The need to enlist parents as partners in helping to create a college-going culture in schools and considerations for fostering parental support for students' preparation for postsecondary education will then be discussed. A description of one school-community-university partnership that increased minority enrollments in advanced level classes from 628 to 2,066 enrollments in five years and low socioeconomic student enrollments in advanced level secondary courses from 315 to 2,678 enrollments in six partner schools will then be shared.

Increasing Access and Success in Postsecondary Education

A gap in the pursuit of postsecondary education exists for students from low socioeconomic groups compared to students from high socioeconomic groups with only one in three (34 percent) of these students pursuing postsecondary education while four of five (80 percent) of students from high socioeconomic groups pursue postsecondary education (National Commission on the High School Senior Year, 2001). Another indicator of a need for a significant change to be made in the level and quality of work achieved by secondary students includes the current discrepancy between the 70 percent of secondary students who enroll in college with one-third never enrolling again after the first semester, and half never graduating (Swail & Perna, 2002).

The Importance of Course Taking Patterns to College Access and Success

Taking advanced level secondary courses is of more importance than grade point average or class rank in determining a student's success in postsecondary education (Adelman, 1999). However, according to the College Board Advanced Placement Report to the Nation (2006), there is a gap between white and Hispanic and African American students in participation in advanced level secondary courses. The report further notes,

> African American, Latino, and Native American students have been traditionally underrepresented in AP courses, and no state with large numbers of African American or Native American students has yet succeeded at providing AP opportunities that allow for equitable representation of these students. (10)

Differences also occur by socioeconomic groups with low socioeconomic students participating in advanced level secondary courses at a much lower percentage than students from high socioeconomic groups (Adelman, 1999; Candara & Maxwell-Jolly, 1999; College Board, 1999, 2006). Parents from high socioeconomic groups influence the placement of their children in advanced level courses to a much greater degree than do parents of low socioeconomic groups (Noguera & Wing, 2006). Useem (1992) found that parents from low socioeconomic groups seldom questioned students' math levels of courses whereas parents of high socioeconomic groups influenced a higher math placement. The New York ACORN Schools Office (1996) found that counselors were more likely to encourage students of high socioeconomic groups to take advanced level courses than students from low socioeconomic groups.

Benefits of Advanced Courses

Studies have clearly shown academic gains resulting for high school students who participate in more rigorous coursework (Borman, Stringfield, & Rachuba, 2000; Candara & Maxwell-Jolly, 1999; Potter & Morgan, 2002; Rothschild, 1999; Santoli, 2002, Stephens, 1999). Kulik's (1992) meta-analysis of research literature revealed achievement gains from two to twenty-three months for students who participated in more rigorous courses as compared with students of corresponding achievement and academic levels of students who participated in regular track courses. Gamoran (1992) similarly found, in a study of twenty thousand ninth graders, that those in more rigorous courses made greater achievement gains. Differential access to learning opportunities is impacted by the availability and access to advanced level courses (Adelman, 1999; Santoli, 2002; Stephens, 1999; Tierney, 2006).

This access influences academic outcomes of the student body. In addition, these disparities in participation in advanced level courses influence college admission test scores with students scoring higher on college admission tests when advanced level courses were taken in secondary school (Adelman, 1999; Santoli, 2002). Assisting all students in receiving a high quality education to ensure both equity and excellence is critical (Scheurich & Skrla, 2003). Many schools, however, are largely ineffective in meeting the needs of high academic achievement throughout a diverse student body (Noguera & Wing, 2006).

As Noguera (2003) argued, "As long as we are able to convince ourselves that simply providing access to education is equivalent to providing equal opportunity, we will continue to treat failing schools as a non-issue" (15). Sanders, Epstein, and Connors-Tadros (1999) stressed,

> Every child has the capacity to succeed in school and in life. Yet, far too many children especially from poor and minority families are placed at risk by school practices that are based on a sorting paradigm in which some students receive high expectations instruction while the rest are relegated to lower quality education and lower quality futures. (iii)

Outreach is needed to influence participation in advanced level courses by a diverse student body (Noguera, 2003).

Parents as Partners for a College-Going Culture

As educators, it is important to recognize that parental involvement takes many forms and that we, as educators, can help to foster that involvement whether it be participation at school events or conversations with the child about his or her future (Hoover-Dempsey, Walker, Sandler, Whetsel, Green, Wilkins, & Closson, 2005; McNeal, 1999; Scribner, Young, & Pedroza (1999). In Noguero and Wing (2006), Noguero's personal account of his life helps to illustrate this:

> As the second of six children from working-class Caribbean immigrant parents, neither of whom graduated from high school or attended college, I benefited from having learned at an early age to understand the importance of education. (12)

Without external support of private tutors, Noguero's parents influenced him and his five siblings' attendance at highly regarded universities. As he shared,

> As new immigrants, my parents rejected the idea that skin color and culture made us racially inferior. We were taught that character and hard work mattered more than race, and that none of the White children we went to school with were inherently superior. Ours is a success story, one of immigrants who are able to reap the rewards of American opportunity through hard work

and determination. Yet, such stories do not negate the fact that, without a Herculean effort, the vast majority of those who are born poor, stay poor. (12)

Noguero's account illustrates that parental involvement in a child's education is highly personal.

Oakes and Lipton (2003) from their work with a Futures project, a project designed to help Latino and African American students of low income to navigate the pathway for college, reported positive benefits that accrued from bridging between the home and school stating, "When schools integrate parents into the work of the school, other parents gain confidence and competence. Such respectful links between home and school help students develop academically, socially, and personally" (415). Oakes and Lipton further stressed, "Steady attention to relationships makes it safe for people to trust one another" (420).

Recognition theory suggests that individuals need to receive a positive reflection by others rather than to be left alone (Kerr, 1997). For parents to be true partners in a child's education, outreach that extends beyond merely inviting parents to school functions is important. Multiple forms of outreach are needed (Pena, 2000). To be true partners in the child's education, Pena recommends, "Despite any social class and cultural differences, teachers and parents must truly value each other as each has knowledge and expertise to contribute" (52). Higher-performing schools "focus efforts to engage families and community members in developing trusting and respectful relationships" (Henderson & Mapp, 2002, 13). Distrust (Lightfoot, 1978), equity traps of deficit thinking (McKenzie & Scheurich, 2004), and feelings of alienation (Oakes, Rogers, & Lipton, 2006) can lower the participation of low-income or minority parents.

Considerations for Fostering Involvement

Parent involvement takes many forms (Melissa, 2001; Morocco, Brigham, & Aguilar, 2006; Scribner, Young, & Pedroza, 1999). The level of discourse concerning the child's future, monitoring of the child's time in completing school work, and helping with homework have been found to be more important to the child's success than whether the parent is a volunteer at school or regularly participates in school functions (Finn, 1998; Wang, Haertel, & Walberg, 1993). In a study of ten migrant families, the children from families that regularly engaged in conversation about the child's future and the importance of education were more successful in school than those children whose families infrequently engaged in conversations about the child's future (Clark, 1983).

Ho and Willms (1996), in a study of NELS: 88 data, a ten-year-long data set, found that volunteering at school activities and attending school activities were not as important as a parent talking with the child and helping plan his or her educational program in influencing higher grades. When planning ways to involve low socioeconomic African American or Hispanic parents, generalizations can impede progress and become excuses for an expectation of low involvement. For low socioeconomic parents, participating in school activities may not be possible due to work responsibilities (Thompson, 2007). Tierney (2006) acknowledged, "Some parents are bystanders or even negative influences" (141). However, a parent's desire for the best for his or her child is not a characteristic of any one ethnic or socioeconomic group, but is an attitude present in all groups (Henderson & Mapp, 2002).

Involvement of low-income and minority parents can be influenced by the school's actions (Henderson & Mapp, 2002; Scribner, Young, & Pedroza, 1999). Scribner and Reyes (1999) found high expectations for parent involvement in Texas valley schools of high Hispanic student and faculty populations. In these schools, minority parents were strong partners in the schools. However, some parents desire involvement with the school, but are unsure how (Pena, 2000). In California, through a project with University of California Los Angeles (UCLA), minority parents of low socioeconomic groups learned ways to monitor the schools' effectiveness and to navigate the system, becoming important partners in the push for excellence and equity (Oakes, Rogers, & Lipton, 2006).

In New York, parents of low socioeconomic groups joined together in an organization called ACORN and participated in research to discern discriminatory practices of schools (New York ACORN, 1996). Parents from low socioeconomic groups repeatedly failed to receive the same recognition or respect of those of higher socioeconomic groups. Opportunities were not provided for open discourse or genuine recognition of the parent's right to influence actions of the school. Paternalistic attitudes prevailed (New York ACORN, 1996). To promote true partnerships in schools, the ACORN organization's recommendations included "end[ing] racist treatment of parents and aggressively promote parent inquiries and involvement" (20–22). The recommendations reinforced the importance of acts of acknowledgement and confirmation of parents.

Bingham (2001) expressed, "Only with face-to-face experience between self and other can the unanticipatible nature of selves be confirmed" (81). Bingham added, "Recognition always takes place within a larger horizon of socially imbued discourses, and those discourses are circumscribed by social power, institutional constraints, and hegemonic norming" (88). In the New York ACORN (1996) study of parent involvement as well as Oakes, Rogers, and Lipton's (2006) study of parents and schools, issues of power prevailed.

The East Texas Gaining Early Awareness and Readiness for Undergraduate Programs (GEAR UP) project was a federally funded effort that assisted six school districts in achieving the structural, cultural, and instructional changes that fostered increased student participation in academically challenging secondary courses that opened the doors to postsecondary education. The East Texas GEAR UP project was designed to provide systemic practices and to support student's academic success. Over 50 percent of the students in each of the middle and high schools in these districts were from low socioeconomic groups. Conceived as a systemic change effort, this project provided over a five-year period direct services to students in grades 7–11, targeted professional development to faculty and staff, community and business involvement, and parental engagement (Alford, 2005).

The East Texas GEAR UP project established a systemwide mindset of high academic expectations for all students to foster increased numbers of secondary students to participate and succeed in advanced level courses in order to prepare them for success in postsecondary education. The project was designed to address the urgent need to increase the college-going and success rates of students in project academic courses. A vital component in improving educational attainment of secondary students was leadership through ongoing communication with parents and students of the importance of the goals and targeted practices and processes to increase the participation and success of secondary students in advanced level classes (Alford, 2005).

Cultural assumptions can prevent discourse and can simply reiterate prejudices or stereotypes (Bingham, 2001). As Bingham stressed, "Prejudice and social constraint may go unspoken when recognition is couched in monolithic terms when the one recognizing remains unavailable for comment or gives simplistic instruction" (129). Instead, regular, open communication with parents is needed that engages parents as partners in the educational process.

Final Reflections

Recognition moves beyond the reiteration of stereotypes. Historical discourses and cultural scripts from the past can limit the present (Bingham, 2001). Instead of providing excuses for lack of outreach to parents, authentically reaching out to all parents as partners in educational process is needed. The time to move forward in enlisting parents as partners for a college-going culture in secondary schools is now.

References

Adelman, C. (1999). Answers in the toolbox: Academic intensity, attendance patterns, and bachelor's degree attainment. *U.S. Department References of Education. Office of Educational Research and Improvement.* Washington, DC: U.S. Government Printing Office.

Alford, B. (2005). Building the capacity to sustain results: The East Texas GEAR UP Project. An East Texas GEAR UP Project Brief. Carthage, TX: Complete Printing.

Bingham, C. W. (2001). *Schools of recognition: Identity politics and classroom practices.* Lanham, MD: Rowman & Littlefield.

Borman, G. D., Stringfield, S., & Rachuba, L. (2000). *Advancing minority high school achievement: National trends and promising programs and practices.* New York: College Board.

Candara, P., & Maxwell-Jolly, J. (1999). *Priming the pump: Strategies for increasing the achievement of underrepresented minority undergraduates.* New York: College Board.

College Board. (2006). *Advanced placement report to the nation: 2006.* Retrieved May 15, 2007, from www.collegeboard.com/prod_downloads/about/news_info/ap/2006/2006_ap-report-nation.pdf

College Board. (1999). *Reaching the top: A report of the national task force on minority high achievement.* New York: College Board.

Clark, R. M. (1983). *Family life and school achievement.* Chicago: University of Chicago Press.

Eccles, J. S., & Harold, R. D. (1993). Parent-school involvement during the early adolescent years. *Teachers College Record, 94*(3), 568–87.

Finn, J. D. (1998). Parental engagement that makes a difference. *Educational Leadership, 55*(8), 20–24.

Gamoran, A. (1992). *Alternative uses of ability grouping: Can we bring high quality instruction to low-ability classes?* Office of Educational Research and Improvement. Madison, WI: Center on Organization and Restructuring of Schools.

Henderson, A. T., & Mapp, K. L. (2002). *A new wave of evidence: The impact of school, family and community connections on students' achievement.* Austin, TX: National Center of Family & Community Connections with Schools: Southwest Educational Development Laboratory.

Ho, E. S., & Willms, J. D. (1996). Effects of parental involvement on eighth grade achievement. *Sociology of Education, 69*(2), 126–41.

Hoover-Dempsey, K. V., Walker, J. M. T., Sandler, H. M, Whetsel, D., Green, C. L., Wilkins, A. S., & Closson, K. (2005). Why do parents become involved?: Research findings and implication. *Elementary School Journal, 106*(2), 105–30.

Kerr, D. (1997). Toward a democratic rhetoric of schooling. In J. I. Goodlad & T. J. McMannon (Eds.), *The public purpose of education and schooling* (73–83). San Francisco: Jossey-Bass.

Kulik, J. A. (1992). An analysis of the research on ability grouping: Historical and contemporary perspectives. *Ability grouping: Research-based decision making series.* Sponsoring agent: Office of Educational Research and improvement, National Research Center on the Gifted and Talented, 9204, 1–72.

Lightfoot, S. L. (1978). *Worlds apart: Relationships between families and schools.* New York: Basic Books.

McKenzie, K. B., & Scheurich, J. J. (2004). Equity traps: A useful construct for preparing principals to lead schools that are successful with racially diverse students. *Educational Administration Quarterly, 40*(5), 601–32.

McNeal, R. B. (1999). Parental involvement as social capital: Different effectiveness on science achievement, truancy and dropping out. *Social Forces, 78*(1), 44–117.

Melissa, M. J. (2001). Does the shoe fit?: Testing models of participation for African-American and Latino involvement in local politics. *Urban Affairs Review, 37*(2), 227–48.

Morocco, C. C., Brigham, N., & Aguilar, C. M. (2006). *Visionary middle school: Signature practices and the power of local invention.* New York: Teachers College Press.

National Commission on the High School Senior Year. (2001). *Raising our sights: No high school senior left behind.* Princeton, NJ: Woodrow Wilson National Fellowship Foundation.

Ndura, E., Robinson, M., & Ochs, G. (2003). Minority students in high school advance placement courses: Opportunity and equity denied. *American Secondary Education, 32*(1), 21–38.

New York ACORN. (1996). *Secret Apartheid: A report on racial discrimination against black and Latino parents and children in the New York City public school.* Retrieved June 20, 2004, from www.acorn.org/ACORNarchives/studies/secretapartheid

Noguera, P. A. (2003). *City schools and the American dream.* New York: Teachers College Press.

Noguera, P. A., & Wing, J. Y. (2006). *Unfinished Business: Closing racial achievement gap in our schools.* San Francisco: Jossey-Bass.

Oakes, J., & Lipton, M. (2003). *Teaching to change the world* (Second Ed.). New York: McGraw-Hill.

Oakes, J., Rogers, J., & Lipton, M. (2006). *Learning power: Organizing for education and justice.* New York: Teachers College Press.

Olivézes, P. A. (2006). Urban students, social ecologies, Part II. In W. Tierney & J. Colyar (Eds.), *Urban high school students and the challenge of access* (71–82). New York: Peter Lang Publishing.

Pena, D. C. (2000). Parent involvement: Influencing factors and limitations. *Journal of Educational Research, 94*(1), 42–54.

Plank, S. B., & Jordan, W. J. (1997). *Reducing talent loss: The impact of information, guidance, and actions on postsecondary enrollment* (Report No. 9). Baltimore: Johns Hopkins University Center for Research on the Education of Students Placed At Risk.

Potter, L., & Morgan, L. (2002). Improve your advanced placement program: What one high school did. *American Secondary Education, 29*(2), 2–8.

Rothschild, E. (1999). Four decades of the advanced placement program. *History Teacher, 32*(2), 175–206.

Sanders, M. G., Epstein, J. L., & Connors-Tadros, L. (1999). *Family partnerships with high school: The parents' perspective.* Washington, DC: Office of Educational Research and Improvement.

Santoli, S. P. (2002). Is there an advanced placement advantage? *American Secondary Education, 30*(3), 23–35.

Scheurich, J. J., & Skrla, L. (2003). *Leadership for equity and excellence.* Thousand Oaks, CA: Corwin Press.

Scribner, J. D., & Reyes, P. (1999). Creating learning communities for high-performing Hispanic students: A conceptual framework. In P. Reyes., J. D. Scribner, & A. P. Scribner (Eds.), *Lessons from high-performing Hispanic schools* (188–210). New York: Teachers College Press.

Scribner, J. D., Young, M. D., & Pedroza, A. (1999). Establishing collaborative relationships with parents. In P. Reyes., J. D. Scribner., & A. P. Scribner (Eds.), *Lessons from high-performing Hispanic schools* (36–61) New York: Teachers College Press.

Stephens, A. (1999). California students strike back. *Black Issues in Higher Education, 15*(26), 9–28.

Swail, W. S., & Perna, L. W. (2002). Pre-college outreach programs: A national perspective. In W. G. Tierney & L. S. Hagedorn (Eds.), *Increasing access to college: Extending possibilities for all students* (15–34). Albany: State University of New York.

Thompson, E. G. (2007). Reconceptualizing parent involvement in minority communities: Expanding NCLB to improve student achievement in African American schools. *Journal of School Public Relations, 27*(4), 1–17.

Tierney, W. G. (2006). Conclusion: Cultural biographies and policy-making. In W. Tierney & J. Colyar (Eds.), *Urban high school students and the challenge of access* (135–47). New York: Peter Lang Publishing.

Useem, E. L. (1992). Middle schools and math groups: Parent's involvement in children's placement. *Sociology of Education, 65*(2), 263–79.

Wang, M. C., Haertel, G. O., & Walberg, H. J. (1993). Toward a knowledge base for school learning. *Review of Educational Research, 63*(3), 249–94.

12

Difficult Conversations about Cultural Identity Issues

Sandra Harris

Diversity is reflected everywhere from the demographics of the workplace to the demographics of our schools. This has led to complex relationships among individuals of all ages in varying cultures within the United States. For example, non-Hispanic white Americans who are sixty-five and older comprise nearly 82 percent of the population, with only 6 percent of the population Hispanic and 12 percent representing other races. However, only 58.9 percent of Americans under eighteen are white, while 19.2 percent are Hispanic and 22 percent is comprised of minorities.

In fact, Hispanics and Asians are growing more than ten times the pace of whites who are not Hispanic (El Nasser & Grant, 2005, 1A), while African American and Native American school-age populations are predicted to remain relatively stable (Carter, 2003). At the same time, research has shown that black and Latino students have become more segregated than at any time in the last thirty years (Fears, 2001).

Changes in family structure are also occurring. Today, less than one-fourth of U.S. households are made up of married couples with children under age eighteen; single mothers head 7.2 percent of households; few children have a caregiver at home who does not work outside the home (Trotter, 2001). Poverty is another concern. Nearly one in five children in the United States live in poverty and extreme poverty is becoming more concentrated in some inner cities (Olson, 2000). Our diversity extends from ethnicity, race, and age, to language, sexual preference, gender, and learning styles, and the number of lists just keeps growing.

The widespread cultural changes in demographics in schools have exacerbated the need for the discourse of recognition, "where we understand the formation of identity and the self as taking place in a continuing dialogue and struggle with significant others. And then in the public sphere, where a politics of equal recognition has come to play a bigger and bigger role" (Taylor, 1994, 37). Bingham (2001) wrote of this unique challenge to educators by noting the "most important recognitive question: How can human dignity be acknowledged again and again?" (5). This has educational implications for student identity that must be addressed beginning with educators themselves. After all, it is the educator who "mirrors back" to the student an "affirming sense" of who he is throughout the school day (Bingham, 2001, 34).

With identity and affirming recognition in mind, the purpose of this chapter is to investigate educators' understandings that influence difficult conversations leading to recognition of others with dignity. This discussion will be framed within the topics of understanding self-identity and understanding identity's influence on communication and difficult conversations.

Understanding Self-Identity

Diller and Moule (2005) define *identity* as the "stable inner sense of who a person is, which is formed by the successful integration of various experiences of the self into a coherent self-image" (120). Understanding our own cultural consciousness plays a large part in the formation of the identity in all individuals. Culture is "like the air we breathe in, it is all around us" (Pang, 2005, 37). It is this invisible culture that surrounds us and determines much of our identity, what we value, and how we respond to our life experiences.

How can educators understand children's identity experiences that might differ from ours, if we do not take time to understand our own cultural identity? For this reason, educators must spend time reflecting on their own culture and personal issues. For example, educators should have a clear sense of their identity and their goals in life. Understanding who has influenced them in their life goals and life attainments is important. Additionally, educators who are aware of how they demonstrate their care for others and who are aware of what others perceive as caring behavior are able to develop empathetic relationships with others.

What Cultural Biases Influence My Identity?

Acknowledging personal bias as part of one's identity is not comfortable. Yet all individuals have biases and prejudices. Consider that you are walking down a dark street at night. Count the number of times you become fearful as people walk toward you. Are you afraid when the woman dressed in a suit walks by? Does your heart race a bit faster when the person coming toward you is a young male wearing a torn t-shirt? Are you even more afraid if he is a different race than you? Before you can begin to recognize the value of all others, educators must reflect on their own identity.

In order to communicate with others in a way that acknowledges their value, educators must begin with becoming aware of our own biases. We do this in several ways. But first we must identify the biases that influence our behaviors and what we believe about others. This means that we must examine our intentions and our actions with in-depth reflection. In so doing we become more aware of how we treat faculty, students, and parents in our school. Do we treat each with the same respect that values their inherent human dignity, or do we stereotype those who are different from us with a negative view of their experiences? Do we put a hierarchical value on experiences so that middle-class values are more "right" than those of someone from poverty? When we act on these beliefs in this limited way, we lose the opportunity to see our common experiences and enhance and enrich our lives by valuing our differences.

What Cultural Biases Are Reflected in My School?

Cultural socialization begins in our homes where we are first taught the norms, beliefs, and values of our parents or guardians. By the time children come to school they have already been enculturated into certain behaviors, values, and practices. Then, as young people become adolescents, race becomes a more rigid identity construct and peer groups assume a greater influence over their identities (Phelan, Davidson, & Ya, 1998). As educators it is not for us to de-value any culture, yet, often this conflict is grounded in student cultural identities.

My own memory is very clear of textbooks in use when I was a child. Every picture of the family included a mother, father, son, daughter, and a dog. While forty years ago, this was a common reflection of the perceived culture at the time, even then, it was not my cultural experience. I remember cringing every time we went to a PTA meeting because I knew that my divorced mother, whose last name was different from mine, would be called the wrong name. Today this is very common, but throughout my elementary and high school years, I only knew one other person whose parents were divorced. I did not like feeling different.

Textbooks are still limited in their use of people of color. For example, in telling America's story of settling the West, Native Americans are rarely presented with a full acknowledgement of their contributions to an understanding of ecology. High school students are still reading Shakespeare, but are less likely to read the Chicano classic by Rudolfo Anaya, *Bless Me, Ultima*. Students from Asian cultures are told "look at me when I talk to you" even though their culture considers this inappropriate. We look to athletes as school heroes, rather than the academically gifted. Femininity is often defined by cheerleaders. Middle-school girls who want to be scientists quit taking advanced sciences by the tenth grade. Noguera (2005) noted, "African American males are more likely than any other group to be subjected to negative forms of treatment in school" (63). All of this has a strong impact on student identity.

Because educators within the school setting contribute much to a student's identity, educators must conduct self-inquiry on themselves to understand their own identities and their own biases.

However, they must also evaluate the policies and actions of the school to identify established or institutional biases. Simply by investigating groups in school, educators can identify if all students are represented or if the groupings in the school are reinforcing a status quo that segregates by gender or ethnicity. I visited a school district recently that has 32 percent population of ethnic diversity of black, Hispanic, and Asian students. Yet nearly every extracurricular club in the school was primarily Anglo. In this same district, which had a balanced gender population, nearly all of the students in the advanced physics class were male.

This same lack of equity involvement extends to parents and the larger community. When students of all races are not involved in the school, neither are their parents. Community businesses that partner with the school reflect this same lack of diversity. In the same district with the 32 percent population of ethnic diversity, there was discussion about what could be done to encourage a more diverse population of parents to attend parent-teacher functions. Within this district there is a dilemma that will not change until institutional cultural biases in current policies and procedures are identified. When parents become involved, students become involved, and when students become involved, parents become more involved.

Understanding Identity's Influence on Communication and Difficult Conversations

Freire (1990) argued, "If I do not love the world—if I do not love life—if I do not love [human beings]—I cannot enter into dialogue" (78). This led Bartlett (2005) to conduct a study in Latin America that explored the respectful relationship between teachers and students that allowed for student autonomy and was built upon student knowledge. She found that often teachers had difficulty valuing students' knowledge in light of teacher goals of socializing students "into their own way of seeing the world" (357).

Bartlett (2005) reported that school-based family intervention programs did not communicate a respect for Mexican parents' cultural perspectives and economic circumstances and this led to damaging educational opportunities for the children. Understanding what influences one's own identity is a precursor to understanding the identity of others. This understanding must be reflected in the conversations of culturally responsive educators.

Hermes (2005) studied teachers working in Native American schools. She observed that most teachers considered the problem of poverty to be a much "more prohibitive factor to school success than culture" (101). This led Hermes to consider identity politics, the internalized idea that "some identities are more valuable than others" (111), and acknowledged that this can be an artifact of racism. By engaging in this conversation, she noted that these judgments, which often climbed to the surface in unconscious judgment before this, are now recognized as such. Consequently, today she notes the importance of acknowledging "that working across differences is always a work in progress" (113).

Noguera (2005) describes a situation at a Bay Area high school where students were required to write a paper on Mark Twain's *Huckleberry Finn* in a college preparatory course. Several black students dropped the class because they objected to the use of the word "nigger" throughout the novel and were told by the teacher not to make an issue of it. Another black male student said that he would just "tell the teacher what she wanted to hear," while a black female student "wrote a paper that focused on race and racial injustice, even though she knew it might result in her being penalized by the teacher" (64–65). Noguera pointed out that this type of experience is where identity and school practices and academic performance intersect. When there is no opportunity for discussion and dialogue, no opportunity to engage in a difficult conversation, the experience often only exacerbates negative identity issues.

Communication in a Global Society Doctoral Class

In the springs of 2006 and 2007, I developed and taught a doctoral-level class called "Communication in a Global Society" in a university in southeast Texas. The purpose of this class was to examine communication within a cultural framework and the impact this has on education leaders who were taking the class. Thirty-three students in two doctoral-level cohorts participated in the class;

eight were male and twenty-five were female. Eight students were African American, while twenty-five students were Caucasian. All students were educational leaders working full-time in a variety of roles, which included superintendent, principal, assistant principal, educational service center director, K–12 lead teacher, community college teacher, and counselor.

One of the assignments in the class required students to write a paper about their understanding of their own identity and how they perceived this affected their communication with students and others in the school setting. Students also wrote weekly reflections about difficult conversations that needed to take place or were taking place on their campus. Much of the following discussion has been drawn from the comments and writings of these students.

Using constant-comparative methods to analyze student comments, I read through all papers several times and coded emerging themes. After my initial readings, a university colleague followed the same procedure and we reviewed the themes that emerged for consistency. This strengthened the reliability of the emergent categories.

Three themes emerged as educational leadership students wrote reflections regarding difficult conversations about cultural identity issues. These themes included the complexity of having difficult conversations, why difficult conversations are important, and the result of having difficult conversations.

The Complexity of Having Difficult Conversations

Every one of the thirty-three students participating in this class in the springs of 2006 and 2007 noted the tremendous difficulty of having difficult conversations in the class itself. In the words of one student, "Real discussions about social justice, race, and even some religious topics are difficult to conduct because they raise emotions to a dangerous level."

Difficult Conversations for Adults

During our class sessions, students talked about how difficult it was for principals and teachers to discuss diversity issues on their campuses. This led a student to note that at the beginning of the class that he "felt a loss of control. I feel like I've been tossed out of a boat into the water, and now I have to tread like crazy or drown." This student went on to say that "it is exciting and bewildering all at the same time. I am thinking about all types of new 'what if's.' The first 'what if' is, What if I can't do this?"

Doctoral students agreed that too often when these difficult conversations did not take place, problem teachers were allowed to continue teaching. For example, one principal shared how a teacher of thirty-eight years continues to teach as though she is still teaching "little white middle-class kids." The reality is that her students are much more diverse and "not at all middle class," consequently, he wondered if they were being taught at all because "she does not know how to teach an ethnically diverse group of kids."

Because what happens at school influences a child's identity as Diller and Moule (2005) have suggested, educators must consider if they see children who are "different" in some way being treated unfairly. If so, do we respond as we know we should? Doctoral students commented how difficult it was to discuss these issues with other staff members. Although, one doctoral student suggested, the challenge should be "to offer compassion rather than condemnation to the person in need" before they can be engaged in meaningful difficult conversations about cultural diversity.

The Effect on Students

Bartlett (2005) noted the importance of valuing student knowledge. Yet, as doctoral students in my class acknowledged the difficulty of conducting cultural conversations, they also noted that they had students who spoke to them about their frustration when encountering racism. These junior high or high school students often still saw themselves as the victims of racism and discrimination. One doctoral student, a principal at a junior high school, pointed out: "Sadly, many of their perceptions may not be unfounded." The class agreed that it was important to let students express themselves and to listen to them. As educators we must defuse what we can, work toward achieving more equitable environments, and also point out how important it is for these students not to treat others in the way they perceive they have been treated.

One doctoral student, a school superintendent, wrote about an experience he had in the late 1970s as a high school student with a black classmate who was "part of the group." Until our class conversations about difficult conversations, he felt he had been given insight into the black culture because of this friendship. Now, he felt that he had missed an opportunity. He wrote that the black student had come "into our culture, learned it, and was ultimately successful as a black man in a white world. We never entered his culture or learned much about it." Today, as a result of the reflective nature, and in-depth discussion of critical cultural issues, he believed that his black high school friend had "spoken the true word in a way I could not hear clearly at the time." Educators cannot hear clearly what a student is saying unless they are able to move away from stereotypical bias and enlarge their understandings of cultural diversity.

Why Difficult Conversations Are Important

All of the doctoral students participating in this class commented about the importance of having difficult conversations. A high school teacher noted that she was trying "to be more open to the concept of prejudice versus racism. Reading about it didn't really make sense until we began to dialogue about it in class." This student noted some of the differences she had in working with a colleague of a different ethnicity. After taking this class she wondered "if I could work more effectively with her now." Another student likened the importance of communication to the saying about *location*. We often hear that *location is everything*. Instead she felt that we should be saying: "communication, communication, communication . . . communication is everything."

Difficult Conversations Identify Cultural Norms

As students engaged in deep dialogue about cultural diversity, they began to reflect on the importance, as one principal said, of "gaining access to another culture." For many of the Caucasian doctoral students this was the first time that they had begun to think about their own white cultural identity. Openly, they began to address the notion that they had a set of cultural norms that influenced their behavior, decisions, and perceptions of the world. This led these leaders to understand the importance of how their perceptions created a culture of leadership and a school climate that was largely a reflection of their particular culture. As one superintendent wrote, "In a larger sense, I began to understand that the leader's own cultural identity and patterns of responding must be evaluated as part of the 'formula' for leading schools properly."

While white students in the beginning of the class had resisted the notion of white privilege, after listening to experiences recounted by students of other ethnicities and invited guest speakers, they began to understand the influence of this privilege on their lives and on the lives of those from other cultures. One assistant principal wrote:

> I used to believe that minority races had the same opportunities that I have; they just had to work as hard as I did. Contrary to that belief I now understand that the system is not designed with minorities in mind. The system is designed for me, the majority culture.

For the first time in their lives, students acknowledged that these difficult conversations had "awakened a level of awareness" of the importance of cultural issues. Several commented that perhaps prior to these conversations they had purposely suppressed the thought processes relative to culture because it made them uncomfortable. Now doctoral students were more comfortable acknowledging their cultural ignorance of all cultures different from their own. They began asking themselves about what it meant to be white or black or Hispanic or Asian in America today. What had been unimportant before to students now had become important because they knew that, as one student wrote, "Other ethnic groups must consider the effect of their race on their lives and, therefore, ethnic self-identification becomes part of the persona."

Difficult Conversations Enhance Identity Recognition

A high school principal compared the notion of difficult conversations and the importance of recognition by quoting from

Shakespeare (*Romeo and Juliet*, act II, scene ii, lines 40–45): "What's Montague? It is nor hand, nor foot, nor arm, nor face, nor any other part belonging to a man. O, be some other name! What's in a name?" He noted the Bible verse (John 1:1): "In the beginning was the Word, and the Word was with God, and the Word was God. And the Word was made flesh, and dwelt among us." Then he quoted Freire, "The essence of dialogue itself: the word" (1990, 75). This student continued to write:

> I find no accident that a diverse group of writers spanning over a thousand years all point to the importance of naming the world, the power of the word. He who names the world defines the culture. And those who are outside of the dialogue are left to find their place instead of defining their placing. One cannot underestimate the power of the word to create, destroy, or remain idle. Engaging in difficult conversations is an example of reaffirming recognition of identity.

As students in this doctoral class engaged in deep conversations about cultural diversity, they identified the importance of cultural norms for themselves and others. Through this process they also reflected on how closely cultural understandings are entwined with personal issues of self-identity that lead to recognition identity with dignity for all.

Result of Engaging in Difficult Conversations

Students agreed that participating in this class was important because it fostered awareness and an urgency of the need for engaging themselves and others in difficult conversations. At the same time, students noted that they began to become more comfortable engaging in difficult conversations.

Awareness and Urgency to Engage in Difficult Conversations

In most cases, doctoral students voiced that this level of awareness had not been present before with the same sense of urgency they shared now. Several students commented that prior to this class, the notion of difficult conversations had been "an under the surface need." Now they realized the urgency. Awareness led one superintendent to note that over the past two years, she had served on a school board with African American members. She wrote:

> I have seen the distress in their eyes as they hear the annual ac-
> countability report and the achievement gaps are highlighted. I
> am now acutely aware of how these members feel as children of
> color underachieve while our efforts to recruit minority teachers
> are only marginally successful.

Now she committed to begin holding "discussions with school leaders and minority members about how to close this gap in this school year."

Although one student, a principal, admitted that he often felt "like a human buffer zone at school," still, participating in these difficult conversations brought cultural identity issues and the important role that adult educators have in this process to the forefront. Consequently, all teachers noted they felt "better equipped" to help students.

Becoming Comfortable with Uncomfortable Conversations

Doctoral students noted that difficult conversations about cultural issues are frightening for many reasons. We saw this because sometimes, even in the controlled environment of our doctoral classroom, discussions became heated. But because students had also built strong, affirming relationships we were able to understand the passion and emotion that led to a disagreement. However, in many cases, educators are not able to have these conversations in a risk-free environment and, thus, they are silent, because they are afraid of hurting another's feelings by saying the wrong thing. This often happens because, as one student noted, "[We are] ignorant of the things our society has really communicated to the black or Hispanic man."

However, the doctoral students in this class, regardless of their ethnicity or cultural background, noted that they became more comfortable when engaging in these difficult conversations, or at the very least as one student wrote, "*somewhat* more comfortable talking about the sensitive issues of cultural differences now."

Being able to discuss race and racial differences led to gaining "a community feeling in our classroom," wrote one student. This student noted that "we are beginning to see the peeling away of the onion skin layers and getting to more inner feelings and thoughts."

As students engaged in difficult conversations the proverbial elephant "definitely began to be moved out of the room and began to be pushed out of the way." This allowed the enlightenment of what students had in common to "come to the surface as differences became less noticeable. As barriers were broken a more comfortable zone began to replace the old barriers," noted one student. This brought new insights to the students in the class regarding "the depth of thought and character of my classmates." While all students agreed that discussion of racial issues was seldom pleasant, they steadfastly agreed that it was "reaffirming to be part of a group that can speak honestly without hostility." Being able to speak honestly helped students achieve a level of comfort even when having uncomfortable or difficult conversations. As a class we called this "getting comfortable with being uncomfortable."

Recognition of Others with Dignity through Difficult Conversations

Philosopher Jean-Paul Sartre pointed out that a distinctive feature of existentialist thought included the idea that a person's identity is not formed by nature or culture. He posited that to "exist" is to constitute an identity, thus what makes someone who he is, is not fixed by what type of person he is, but what he makes of himself (Crowell, 2006). While this may be true for some individuals, for many of the children in our schools, this is not the case.

Much of a young person's identity comes from how they perceive that other family members, peers, and teachers perceive them to be. Too often, as a doctoral student in my class wrote, "They are left to find their place, instead of defining their placing." How educators perceive students informs their identity. Before we are able to fully understand this phenomenon, we must understand our own identity and its influence on our institutions. It follows, that in so doing, we begin to understand how our actions influence students and, thus, how important it is for educators to engage in difficult, self-reflective conversations.

Participating in conversations in our doctoral classes that "peel away the layers" of identity resonates with the hope that when adult students go back to their own school campuses, they will be more able to engage other educators in these complex, deep conversations. As one student wrote, "Perhaps by understanding my own identity and how I influence students, I can better understand those who might be different from me . . . perhaps this will allow me to be open to ways that we are also alike."

This chapter purposed to investigate educators' understandings of difficult conversations leading to recognition of others with dignity. Overall, students who participated in a doctoral class with this as its focus determined that difficult conversations about cultural identity are hard to hold but critically, even urgently, important to hold. When we provide an opportunity for educators to engage in difficult conversations, we learn more about our own identity and more about the identity of others. At the same time, we develop the ability to become more comfortable in these conversations.

Becoming comfortable with difficult conversations does not mean that we hold these discussions lightly; instead, it simply means that as we engage in deep conversation, we become more able to facilitate deeper, richer conversations about topics that are not easy to discuss—but must be discussed. Otherwise, we do not develop an awareness that leads to deeper, richer understandings. In so doing educational leaders become more adept at meeting the needs of students.

However, there is still a challenge before us. One student identified this in the following way, "Although I feel more ready for these conversations, I fear that many of the teachers at the front line are not ready." Clearly, it is the responsibility of leaders to involve others in these conversations constructively. Thus, as educational leaders better understand ourselves and one another, the charge falls to us to begin a liberating dialogue that will, as one doctoral student said, "shine through the darkness and silence of the past." Participating in the dialogue of cultural identity is one way to accept Bingham's (2001) challenge to address human dignity. After all, we acknowledge human dignity again and again through deep, difficult conversations.

References

Bartlett, L. (2005). Dialogue, knowledge, and teacher-student relations: Freirean pedagogy in theory and practice. *Comparative Education Review, 49*(3), 344–64.

Bingham, C. (2001). *Schools of recognition: Identity politics and classroom practices.* Lanham, MD: Rowman & Littlefield Publishers.

Carter, G. R. (2003). Changes in educational practice. In W. A. Owings & L. Kapling (Eds.), *Best practices, best thinking* (247–53). Thousand Oaks, CA: Corwin Press.

Crowell, S. (2006). Existentialism. The Stanford Encyclopedia of Philosophy. Retrieved July 7, 2007, from plato.stanford.edu/archives/spr2006/entries/existentialism

Diller, J. V., & Moule, J. (2005). *Cultural competence: A primer for educators.* Belmont, CA: Thomson Wadsworth.

El Nasser, H. & Grant, L. (2005, June 9). Immigration causes age, race split. *USA Today,* p. 1A.

Fears, D. (2001, July 18). Schools' racial isolation growing. *Washington Post,* p. A3.

Freire, P. (1990). *Pedagogy of the oppressed.* New York: Continuum.

Hermes, M. (2005). White teachers, native students. In J. Phillion, M. F. He, & F. M. Connelly (Eds.), *Narrative and experience in multicultural education* (95–115). Thousand Oaks, CA: Sage.

Noguera, P. (2005). The trouble with black boys: The role and influence of environmental and cultural factors on the academic performance of African American males. In O. S. Fashola (Ed.), *Educating African American males: Voices from the field* (51–78). Thousand Oaks, CA: Corwin Press.

Olson, L. (2000). High poverty among young makes schools' jobs harder. *Education Week, 20*(4), 34–35.

Pang, V. (2005). *Multicultural education: A caring-centered, reflective approach* (Second Ed.). Boston: McGraw Hill.

Phelan, P. A., Davidson, H., & Ya, C. (1998). *Adolescent worlds.* Albany, NY: SUNY Press.

Taylor, C. (1994). *Multiculturalism: Examining the politics of recognition.* Princeton, NJ: Princeton University Press.

Trotter, A. (2001). Census shows the changing face of U.S. households. *Education Week, 20*(37), 5.

13

Value-Added Community: Recognition, Induction-Year Teacher Diversity, and the Shaping of Identity

John C. Leonard

Teachers on campuses today represent a spectrum of diversity by race, gender, ethnicity, class, sexual identity, religious belief, ability, linguistic groupings, and age. It is a diversity that is frequently segregated and segmented in our schools. Often school leaders tend to focus on the diversity of their students yet fail to understand the importance of recognizing and overcoming cultural barriers serving to neutralize effective collaboration among faculty.

Hill (1995) advocated for a renewed focus on building community in organizations through the strengthening of interpersonal relationships, not by focusing on management structures. School principals play a critical role in leading their staffs in building a sense of community and in honoring the diversity that serves to strengthen a faculty's collaborative bond. Therefore, principals should forge teacher-to-teacher relationships based on improved understandings of diversity and the importance of valuing their school's social capital.

The process of forging a faculty's collaborative bond must include recognition of the importance of diversity during all stages of the employment relationship beginning with teacher recruitment, selection, and induction. The latter induction period is particularly important in view of the perception held by public school leaders that preparation programs are out of touch with the realities of the changing demographics of twenty-first-century schools (Grant, 1994). Kuhn (1962) coined the term "paradigm shift" and indicated that when a paradigm shifts all previously held conventions are neutralized. Although school leaders have seen the demographic shift coming for decades, they have failed to adequately prepare teachers for the accompanying social dynamics attendant to a dramatically different workforce.

Framing the Issue

As the population in the United States has shifted in recent decades, the definition of "diversity" itself has also undergone a transformation. Beyond simple heterogeneity, diversity in the school setting reflects a reality of individuals and groups that are unique across a broad spectrum of demographic and philosophical differences. Teachers on campuses today should be representative of our nation's changing mosaic of diversity by race, sex, ethnicity, class, sexual identity, religious belief, ability, linguistic groupings, and age. School leaders must move beyond a politically correct tolerance of staff diversity and embrace an understanding of the rich contributions a diverse staff contributes to the attainment of school's goal of student success and equity. This concept of diversity empowers a staff to collaborate without anyone being advantaged or disadvantaged by considerations irrelevant to the accomplishment of the organization's mission.

Demographic Shifts

School leaders must be cognizant of the reality of changing demographics and the significant issues that materially influence their organization. As an example, focusing on the singular issue of race as a dimension contained in our broad definition of diversity, Hobbs & Stoops (2002), in a study of U.S. census data found that when all people of races other than white were aggregated, the minority population increased by 88 percent between 1980 and 2000, while the white and non-Hispanic population for the same period grew by only 7.9 percent. All of these changes are indicative of the dramatic shift in racial diversity in America and its schools.

A contributing factor to the lack of understanding of diversity issues in public schools is the continuance of a predominately white and female teacher workforce. Feistritzer (1996) reinforced this homogenate structure stating that nine out of ten public school teachers are white and approximately three in four are female. At a time when minority student enrollments are trending upward, the number of minority teachers is in decline. Sharon Robinson, Educational Testing Service's executive vice-president, in remarks to the National Education Association, indicated that this demographic is not likely to change in the near future (Melley, 2001).

Recent data on teachers in the United States reported the majority of elementary and secondary schoolteachers to be female and white. Presently the teacher population is approximately 87 percent white (American Association of Colleges for Teacher Education [AACTE], 1999) and 74 percent female. Recent estimates indicate that the percentage of white teachers in public schools increased to 90 percent. At the same time, nearly 35 percent of students in classrooms are minority: 64.2 percent white, 16 percent black/African American, 14 percent Hispanic, 3.8 percent Asian/Pacific Islander, and 1 percent American Indian/Alaskan Native (Snyder, 1998).

Statistics of the teacher workforce in public education for the last decade indicate a disturbing discrepancy in the percentages of minority teachers as compared with student demographic changes. Snyder & Hoffman (1994) found that in 1990–1991, 9.2 percent of public elementary and secondary teachers were black/African American, 3.1 percent were Hispanic, and 1 percent were Asian/Pacific Islander. Yet fifty-three million students are enrolled in U.S. elementary and secondary schools with 35 percent representing ethnic or racial minority groups. This trend is expected to continue during the twenty-first century with minority groups being the majority in American schools by 2050 (Futrell, Gomez, & Bedden, 2003).

However, diversity issues center around more than just issues of gender and race. Schools have never been culturally "neutral" and teachers are charged with laying the cultural foundations needed for excellence and equity (Broekhuizen & Dougherty, 1999). National organizations have continued to stress the importance of having a diverse teacher workforce to provide role models for both minority and majority students (Lewis, 1996). Clearly, pluralism has taken on an expanded definition beyond ethnicity in our schools and is reflective of our nation's being one of the most diverse in the world. Thus, one of the most pressing issues facing school principals today is the need to prepare our staffs to not only teach students from diverse backgrounds, but also to facilitate a professional environment that fosters a collegial teaching staff of diverse race, sex, ethnicity, class, sexual identity, religious belief, ability, linguistic groupings, and age. Beyond school leaders' building of community and the strengthening of interpersonal relationships on their campus, organizational benefits ensue such as improved teacher retention, particularly with teachers new to the profession.

A distinct understanding of the issues attendant to diversity is particularly important for the principal's support of induction-year teachers. Teachers new to the profession often have minimal training in diversity issues, perhaps as little as the ubiquitous multicultural awareness courses mandated in most university programs. Other teacher education approaches spread issues of diversity throughout the curriculum (Grant, 1994; Zeichner & Hoeft, 1996).

This lack of exposure often results in novice teachers becoming discouraged and resulting in behaviors averse to effective schools such as teacher turnover. Factors such as novice teachers feeling isolated from colleagues, being given difficult working assignments, and experiencing unclear expectations for their own role as a professional run counter to fulfilling the goals of a successful school. School leaders should build their school's capacity for valuing the unique contributions of a diverse staff that will strengthen their school and allow novice teachers to participate in school improvement a meaningful way.

The *Principal* of the Issue

Unity through diversity is the only true and enduring unity.

Former United Nations Secretary-
General Boutros Boutros-Ghali

As school staffs interact with one another, they develop and exchange a diverse set of identities. These identities—including gender, race, ethnicity, culture, sexual orientation, religion, varying physical and mental abilities, class, age, education, profession, and regional identity—carry socially constructed meaning and value. If principals are to be the "mirror" in supervising their staff, then they must act with one very inclusive mirror. Principals can, and should, provide leadership for creating and sustaining campuses conducive to the assimilation and socialization of novice teachers.

The ever-changing demands placed on public schools require a principal's concerted and systematic approach to the creation of an organizational environment that builds on its shared commitment to commonly held beliefs and values the staff as social capital. Cunningham and Cordeiro (2003) stated that social capital involves "the quality of relationships among individuals within an organization and the structures that frame those relationships" (7). This commitment can only be actualized with a principal's clear understanding of how human capital development—a value-added learning community—provides the impetus for meaningful collaboration and contributions within the framework of an effective school.

The following assumptions are made in regard to the development of an inclusive support system for new teachers:

1. The diversity of social capital must be valued in a school organization.
2. In an effective school, teachers engage in a continuous dialogue focused on improving teaching-learning for all students.
3. When collegial relationships are nurtured, veteran staff members demonstrate a greater capacity to support induction-year teachers.
4. The existence of successful collegial relationships serves to motivate and retain teachers.

Cognizance of Social Capital = Value-Added Community

> The failure of hierarchies to solve society's problems forced people to talk to one another—and that was the beginning of networks.
>
> John Naisbitt in *Megatrends*

Cognizance of the importance of social capital requires the principal, through his or her leadership, to accept and "capitalize" on diversity, whether that diversity is associated with gender, race, ethnicity, culture, sexual orientation, religion, varying physical and mental abilities, class, age, education, profession, regional identity, or ideas. Cohen and Prusak (2001) offered a definition of social capital as consisting of the active connections among people sharing a commitment to trust, mutual understanding, and shared values and behaviors. These elements are needed to bind people together into cooperative networks and communities.

In the organizational context of schools, social capital has relevancy because it is these networks and communities, when engaged in the dialogue of school improvement, that will produce a much needed paradigm shift. Naisbitt (1982) defined networking as "people talking to each other, sharing ideas, information and resources" (191). The school organization's finished product is not the critically important aspect of networking; it is, rather, the process of colleagues communicating about teaching and learning—the social capital working collaboratively with the principal in the school improvement process.

Putnam (2000) emphasized another important dimension to the importance of social capital—whether the organization is *bonding* (or exclusive) or *bridging* (or inclusive). Bonding in organizations has the tendency to reinforce exclusive or homogenous groups, while organizations that display a bridging and inclusive nature embrace and include all individuals regardless of the perceived social divide.

The result from a leader's valuing social capital is analogous to a symphony orchestra functioning with, or without, the violin section. With all instrument families present and in "harmony" the orchestra performs with a shared trust and understanding under its conductor based on the cooperative participation of all—as a team. Without a full compliment of instrumentation, the orchestra would never be able to perform the symphonic repertoire and the conductor would, and should be, out of a job. Schools are the same: without the full participation of all teachers—indeed, all stakeholders—the organization will fail to capitalize on its most prized resource—its people.

The goal of inclusion is not possible in a traditionally organized school that is reflective of the inequalities existing in our society. Principals must value the inclusive quality of the relationships among and between teachers regardless of their race, sex, ethnicity, class, sexual identity, religious belief, ability, linguistic groupings, and age. Where social capital is undervalued, there are conflicting values and a substantial lack of trust. For example, in the context of school organization, a lack of social capital can be seen if people have abandoned hope of working in a collaborative environment, where individual goals are advanced in place of the collective, agreed upon goals of the school, and where the quality of relationships among staff at best is superficial and bonding or trusts are absent (North Central Regional Educational Laboratory [NCREL], 1996). Among the benefits Cohen and Prusak (2001) present for valuing social capital include:

- improved knowledge sharing because trust is evident and individuals have common frames of reference and goals;
- maintaining valuable organizational knowledge attributable to reduced turnover rates; and,
- a greater coherence of action due to organization stability and shared understanding.

Certainly, effective principals, either purposely or intuitively, work toward relationships that are inclusive and bridging to the recognized diversity of their staff. When principals strive to improve the conditions for an inclusive school environment the resultant continuous dialogue on school renewal will create a bridge to a quality professional learning community.

One of the most important relationships a principal must address is with a school's induction-year teachers, particularly through the lens of diversity. Often an undervalued resource, teachers new to the profession should be actively assimilated into the school community and engaged in school improvement dialogue. Statistics dramatically underscore the need to support an induction-year teacher as exemplified by the research of Green, Roebuck and Futrell (1994), which indicated that 15 percent will leave after the first year, and up to 50 percent of the beginning teachers will leave before their seventh year; first-year teachers also reported alarming feelings of inadequacy and isolation. Clearly, principals need to examine their leadership and bridging and support strategies for induction-year teachers.

Principals can reverse these disturbing trends by taking a proactive role. A seminal step would be to make cultural diversity a critical component in the school renewal process. In addition, principals must be cognizant of their school's induction-year social capital. In addition to helping teachers understand a diverse student body, school leaders must make the support of new teachers a priority by finding ways to engage them as valued partners in the larger school community. The aggregated social capital of the school, fully participating in the school renewal process, will not only actuate the talents of induction-year teachers, but also serve to build the professional bridges necessary for continuous improvement.

Conclusion

Educators have come a long way in both the recognition of diversity among students and faculty and the need to value all staff in the educational improvement process. If schools are to continue to be successful, they must celebrate and capitalize on the teacher diversity evident in their staff and include in this process their induction-year colleagues.

Principals are key to this success and must value and model schools where every teacher is a full participant in the school-renewal process. In order to accomplish this goal, school leaders should provide an organizational foundation predicated on the inclusion of all staff—including, but not limited to, induction-year teachers. Saravia-Shore and Garcia (2001) argued that every single person in our enormously diverse school organizations has the power to serve as an invaluable resource for all others. When diversity is recognized as a valuable part of a school's social capital and collegial relationships are fostered in a trusting and supportive process, schools will become value-added communities of learners bridging to induction-year teachers.

References

American Association of Colleges for Teacher Education. (1999). Teacher education pipeline: Schools, colleges, and departments of education. Washington, DC: AACTE.

Broekhuizen, L. D., & Dougherty, B. (1999). Teacher diversity: Implications for professional development. *Publication of Pacific Resources for Education and Learning.* Honolulu. Retrieved March 26, 2003, from www.prel.org

Cohen, D., & Prusak, L. (2001). *In good company: How social capital makes organizations work.* Boston: Harvard Business School Press.

Cunningham, W. G., & Cordeiro, P. A. (2003). *Educational leadership: A Problem-based approach.* Boston: Allyn & Bacon.

Feistritzer, C. E. (1996). Profile of teachers in the U.S. Washington DC: National Center for Education Information.

Futrell, M. H., Gomez, J., & Bedden, D. (2003). Teaching the children of the new America: The challenge of diversity. *Phi Delta Kappan, 84*(5), 381–85.

Grant, C. A. (1994). Best practices in teacher preparation for urban schools: Lessons from the multicultural teacher education literature. *Action in Teacher Education, 16*(3), 1–18.

Green, C., Roebuck, J., & Futrell, M. H. (1994). Combating isolation: A first year teacher support program. *Rural Educator, 15*(3), 40–45.

Hill, N. S., Jr. (1995, May–June). Voices for diversity. *Future Teacher, 1*(2), 3.

Hobbs, F., & Stoops, N. (2002, November). Demographic trends in the 20th century: Census 2000 special report. *U.S. Department of Commerce U.S. Census Bureau.* Washington, DC: U.S. Government Printing Office, 71–75.

Kuhn, T. (1962). *The structure of scientific revolutions.* Chicago: University of Chicago Press.

Lewis, M. S. (1996). Supply and demand of teachers of color. Washington, DC: ERIC Clearinghouse on Teaching and Teacher Education. (ERIC Document Reproduction Service ED 390 875).

Melley, C. (2001). ETS's Robinson: Address diversity in tomorrow's workforce today. *Education Testing Service.* Retrieved October 17, 2003, from www.ets.org /search97cgi/s97_cgi

Naisbitt, J. (1982). *Megatrends: Ten new directions for transforming our lives.* New York: Warner Books.

North Central Regional Educational Laboratory (NCREL). (1996, January). School-community collaboration. *New Leaders for Tomorrow's Schools, 2*(1), 19–25. Retrieved May 6, 2006, from http://www.ncrel.org/cscd/pubs/lead21 /2-1a.htm

Putnam, R. D. (2000). *Bowling alone: The collapse and revival of American community.* New York: Simon & Schuster.

Saravia-Shore, M., & Garcia, E. (2001). Diverse teaching strategies for diverse learners. In R. W. Cole, (Ed.), *Educating everybody's children: Diverse teaching strategies for diverse learners* (41–97). Alexandria, VA: Association of Supervision and Curriculum Development.

Snyder, T. (1998). *Digest of education statistics.* Washington, DC: National Center for Education Statistics, Department of Education.

Snyder, T. D., & Hoffman, C. M. (1994). *Digest of education statistics.* Washington, DC: National Center for Educational Statistics, U.S. Department of Education. (ERIC Document Reproduction Service No. ED 377 253).

Zeichner, K., & Hoeft, K. (1996). Teacher socialization for cultural diversity. In J. Sikula, T. Buttery, & E. Guyton (Eds.), *Handbook on research on teacher education* (Second Ed.) (525–54). New York: McMillan.

14

Coda: Recognition, Difference, and the Future of America's Schools

Patrick M. Jenlink

> Once labels are applied to people, ideas about people who fit the label come to have social and psychological effects. In particular, these ideas shape the ways people conceive of themselves and their projects. So the labels operate to mold what we may call identification, the process through which individuals shape their projects—including their plans for their own lives and their conceptions of the good life—by reference to available labels, available identities.
>
> Appiah, 2005, 66

> To further complicate matters, not only do the judgments of others affect an individual's developing identities; it also matters just who those others are. Some people, depending on their social position, have relatively more power and authority, especially in regard to specific identities. However, power is never given but depends very much on the nature of the individuals involved in the encounter.
>
> Danielewicz, 2001, 39

What role might recognition play in the future of America's schools? In large part, the questions of recognition are questions of schooling and of education. And perhaps most important, they are questions of identity and questions of pedagogy and politics. To see how we are obligated as with respect to recognition, we need to reflect on the complex and dynamical nature of identity and the interactions of social identities. Individual identities are multilayered—one's identity is not singular, but rather is comprised of a number of social and cultural identities, such as gender, class, race, ethnicity, sexual orientation, and so forth—and at the same time are defined by hierarchical relationships to others. "Difference" may itself be a product of inequality, and therefore identity and identification disadvantage some while advantaging others.

Arguably the problem of escaping oppressive forms of social recognition—discrimination, marginalization, subordination, and so on—is typically one of liberation from particular forms of recognition, a process that demands the critical scrutiny of social relations, and in the attempt to transform these relations, the withholding of recognition from those aspects of social identities implicated in inequality and injustice. In America's schools, the politics of recognition interprets as a politics of difference. Simply stated, identity becomes a degree of definition dependent in large part on identification with different cultural groups, and how individuals are recognized or not. The politics of recognition is a factor that educators in America's schools can no longer afford to ignore.

Recognition, as a political force and focus of pedagogical practice, is central to identity formation in schools and classrooms. The *circuits of recognition* (Kerr, 1997), which flow through the structures of schooling, are responsible, in part, for identity shaping and identification. The discourses that shape curricular, instructional, and pedagogical practices as well as those cultural discourses that are emblematic of the ideological and political agendas form circuits of recognition. Students, teachers, and other cultural workers interact with each other through circuits of recognition, immersed daily in the discourses.

In turn, these discourses—dominating and dominant—leave ideological inscriptions on the identity of the individuals, shaping identities in relation to cultural patterns and politics. If schools are to become, as Bingham (2001) argues, *schools of recognition*, then there is much work that must be undertaken by educators and other cultural workers. They must work to make the public space of America's schools the site of struggles for recognition that strive not only to protect otherwise neglected minorities, but also to form a discourse of recognition focused on the social meaning of moral and political standards for difference within a democratic society.

This collection of chapters advocates for the individual and his or her recognition. It is important that the authors argue for an understanding of how recognition is used or misused in and through the structures of schooling. By making the case for understanding how recognition plays out in the daily lives of students and teachers and other cultural workers, the authors argue that ultimately school is a place shaped more by the structures of schooling and the cultural inscription of ideological-driven recognition embedded through discourses and practices. The chapters, when taken together, present, in specific relief, a portrait of the *circuits of recognition* that course through the very life of the school.

The purpose that drew the authors of the various chapters in this collection together will be realized when the reader understands that recognition is a social force and at the same time a social responsibility in our democratic society. This force may yield both positive and negative influence in shaping of individual identity and the identification with collective identities. When misrecognition is enacted, a negative force is at work that furthers the tensions of racism, genderism, sexism, and similar ideologically driven actions against those in society that are different or not like us. However, when recognition is enacted that intends to shape identity and affirm an individual, it is a step toward realizing the aims of democracy through embracing difference as a defining quality of a democratic society.

The responsibility we share, as individuals and cultural groups alike, is that of illuminating injustices that hallmark segments of society. The responsibility is to also interrogate the ideologies at work in our society and in our schools and to make visible the politics of identity that otherwise remain hidden and at the same time continue to silence the voices of difference.

References

Appiah, A. K. (2005). *The ethics of identity*. Princeton, NJ: Princeton University Press.

Bingham, C. W. (2001). *Schools of recognition: Identity politics and classroom practices*. Lanham, MD: Rowman & Littlefield.

Danielewicz, J. (2001). *Teaching selves: Identity, pedagogy, and teacher education*. Albany: State University of New York Press.

Kerr, D. (1997). Toward a democratic rhetoric of schooling. In J. I. Goodlad & T. J. McMannon (Eds.), *The public purpose of education and schooling* (73–83). San Francisco: Jossey-Bass.

About the Editors and Contributors

About the Editors

Patrick M. Jenlink is professor of doctoral studies in the Department of Secondary Education and Educational Leadership and director of the Educational Research Center at Stephen F. Austin State University. He earned his B.S. degree with majors in sociology and biology, and his teaching certification in social sciences from Northwestern Oklahoma State University. Dr. Jenlink also earned his M.A. in education with emphasis in counseling from Northwestern Oklahoma State University. His doctorate in educational administration was received from Oklahoma State University. Dr. Jenlink has served as a classroom teacher at the junior high and high school level, with assignments in social sciences and natural sciences, as well as serving as K–12 counselor. He has also served as building administrator and school district superintendent in Oklahoma. His university teaching experience includes Northwestern Oklahoma State University, Western Michigan University, and assignments in Europe with the University of Oklahoma and NATO. Dr. Jenlink's teaching emphasis in doctoral studies at Stephen F. Austin State University includes courses in ethics and philosophy of leadership, research methods and design, and leadership theory and practice. Dr. Jenlink's research interests include politics of identity, democratic education and leadership, and critical theory. He has authored numerous articles, guest edited journals, authored or coauthored numerous chapters in books, and edited or coedited several books. Currently Dr. Jenlink serves as editor of *Teacher Education & Practice* and coeditor of *Scholar-Practitioner Quarterly*, both peer-reviewed journals. His most recent book is *Dialogue as a Collective Means of Design Conversation*. Dr. Jenlink's current book projects include a coauthored book, *Developing Scholar-Practitioner Leaders: The Empowerment of Educators* (forthcoming), and *Dewey's Democracy and Education Revisited: Contemporary Discourses for Democratic Education an Leadership* (forthcoming).

Faye Hicks Townes, a former high school English teacher, is a visiting associate professor with the Center for Partnerships to Improve Education (CPIE) and the Teacher Education Department at the College of Charleston in Charleston, South Carolina. She teaches courses in foundations of education and pedagogy. She also works with teachers and students in underperforming schools to improve writing skills. Her research interests are guided by the impact of gender, poverty, and ethnicity on issues of equity in educational settings. Recent research projects have focused on the self-expression of female adolescents through essays and preservice teachers' perceptions of urban schools. She is a founding member and current treasurer of the National Association of Holmes Scholars Alumni (NAHSA). She has served as associate editor of the journal *Teacher Education and Practice* and guest editor for *Urban Education*.

About the Authors

Betty Alford is currently a full-time professor at Stephen F. Austin State University in the Department of Secondary Education and Educational Leadership. Alford earned her doctoral degree in educational administration in 1996 from the University of Texas at Austin. She has served as a middle school principal, an assistant elementary school principal, a high school counselor, an education service center consultant, and a secondary and elementary teacher. In her work at Stephen F. Austin State University, she currently serves as department chair and doctoral program coordinator and previously served as mid-management program coordinator. She has served as a cowriter for four U.S. Department of Education partnership grants totaling over $10 million dollars. Dr. Alford has presented papers at AERA, UCEA, NCPEA, SERA, College Board National Forum, College Board Regional Institutes, and the GEAR UP National Conference, and she has authored journal articles and book chapters. Her research interests include the study of leadership preparation within the context of a principal preparation or doctoral program for educational leadership, the study of partnerships to develop a college-going culture in secondary schools, and the study of successful practices in meeting the needs of English-language learners.

Julia Ballenger is currently the E. J. Campbell Distinguished Professor and an associate professor in the Department of Secondary Education and Educational Leadership at Stephen F. Austin State University, Nacogdoches, Texas, where she serves as coordinator of the Principal Preparation Program and the Project DEVELOP Grant. Dr. Ballenger earned an M.A. in education in 1973 from Texas A&M University, Commerce, Texas, and a Ph.D. in 1996 from the University of Texas in Austin. Dr. Ballenger's professional experience encompasses the public school, state, and university levels. At the public school level, she served as a teacher, principal, consultant, and central office administrator in both rural and urban school districts. At the state level, she served as a regional director and program coordinator in the accountability and accreditation division of the Texas Educational Agency in Austin. Her research agenda includes gender equity, social justice, principal program evaluation, and culturally responsive pedagogy. She has published and presented various papers and studies at the state and national levels. Dr. Ballenger is actively involved in organizations at the university, state, and national levels. She has served in leadership roles in organizations such as Phi Delta Kappa, American Association of University Women, and the Texas Council of Women School

Executives. At the state level, she has served as president of the Texas Council of Professors of Educational Administration, and at the national level, she currently serves as membership chair for AERA/SIG-RWE, assistant editor for NCEPA Connextions, NCATE-ELCC taskforce member, and NCATE/ELCC program reviewer.

Angela Crespo Cozart is an associate professor at the College of Charleston, Charleston, South Carolina. She is a native Spanish speaker born in Puerto Rico, but she and her family moved to the U.S. mainland shortly before she started her formal K–12 education. Dr. Cozart is a former high school English teacher. She is the English for Speakers of Other Languages (ESOL) program director at her institution. Her main areas of interest are ESOL, culture, and teaching children from diverse backgrounds. She has traveled to Kenya and China with students and teachers. She was the lead teacher during her two trips to China when teachers and students taught English and American culture to Chinese students and teachers. While in Kenya, she helped build a clinic for an orphanage. One of her teaching goals is to help her students, future teachers, to understand the impact of culture on teaching and learning. Dr. Cozart is a member of the National Association of Holmes Scholars Alumni.

Sandra Harris is a former public and private school educator. She is currently professor and director of the Center for Doctoral Studies in Educational Leadership at Lamar University in Beaumont, Texas. Harris is the author of numerous publications. Her books include *BRAVO Principal*, *BRAVO Teacher*, and *Managing Conflict: 50 Strategies for School Leaders*. She has also published three best practices books of award-winning principals at the elementary level, secondary level, and the superintendency. She is president of the National Council of Professors of Educational Administration and the former editor of the *NCPEA Educational Leadership Review Journal*. Her research interests include educational reform, cultural studies, educational leadership, and preparation programs.

Raymond A. Horn Jr. is a retired public school educator and an associate professor of education at Saint Joseph's University in Philadelphia, Pennsylvania. He is the director of the Interdisciplinary Doctor of Education Program for Educational Leaders and the director of educational leadership and professional studies graduate programs. Horn is the author of numerous scholarly publications. His books include *Standards Primer, Understanding Educational Reform: A Reference Handbook,* and *Teacher Talk: A Post-Formal Inquiry into Educational Change.* He is the coeditor of *The Praeger Handbook of Education and Psychology,* and *American Standards: Quality Education in a Complex World—The Texas Case.* In addition, he is the coeditor of the scholarly journal *Scholar-Practitioner Quarterly.* His research interests include educational reform, critical theory, cultural studies, curriculum studies, and educational leadership. The theme that guides his research is educational change within the postmodern context and the promotion of socially just, caring, and democratic educational systems.

John Leonard is an associate professor in educational leadership at Stephen F. Austin State University. Prior to joining the SFASU faculty, he was employed for twenty-nine years as a public school teacher, assistant principal, high school principal, assistant superintendent, and superintendent of schools. Leonard earned a B.A. in music education from Southwest Texas State University, a M.S. in music education from the University of Illinois, and a Ph.D. in educational leadership from Texas A&M University, College Station. Leonard's instructional responsibilities at Stephen F. Austin State University include teaching in the principal and superintendent preparation programs and the doctoral program. His primary areas of interest are organizational management, human resource management, and school community relations. In 2005 he received the Teaching Excellence Award for the Department of Secondary Education and Educational Leadership. In addition to teaching, Dr. Leonard has served the College of Education as interim associate dean for academic affairs with primary responsibilities for NCATE accreditation and curriculum management. Leonard serves on the Dean's Advisory Council and is editor of the College of Education's Annual Report. Research interests for Dr. Leonard are in the areas of school leadership, organizational management, and arts education.

Vincent E. Mumford is an associate professor in the Department of Physical Education and Sport in the Herbert H. and Grace A. Dow College of Health Professions, at Central Michigan University. He is the executive director of the Center for Global Sport Leadership. Dr. Mumford received his doctorate from the University of Delaware in Educational Leadership, where he studied as a Holmes Scholar. He has a diverse professional background with experience in academics, administration, and athletics as a participant, teacher, coach, and administrator at various levels. He has received many honors and awards including the American Red Cross Michigan Heroes Award, Volunteers are Central Award, and Outstanding Mentor of the Year. He is a leading expert in sport administration and leadership. He has been appointed to numerous committees and advisory boards, including *Athletic Management*, the YMCA, and the National Football League (NFL). He is frequently called upon to consult or speak on various subjects such as gender equity, strategic planning, sales, marketing and promotions, fund raising, facility design and operation, event management, and leadership.

Amanda M. Rudolph is an assistant professor in the Department of Secondary Education and Educational Leadership at Stephen F. Austin State University in Nacogdoches, Texas. She is the author of *Techniques in Classroom Management* as well as articles on classroom management and teacher education. She also serves as assistant editor for *Teacher Education and Practice*. Her research interests include classroom management for preservice teachers, online teaching and learning, arts education, and educational change and reform.

Kris Sloan is an assistant professor in the School of Education at St. Edward's University in Austin, Texas. He also teaches at the Massachusetts College of Liberal Arts in the Summer Leadership Academy for K–12 Administrators. Dr. Sloan has worked as a curriculum designer and has taught in the United States, the Philippines, and Colombia. He is the author of numerous journal articles and book chapters on issues related to teacher education and the ways accountability-related curriculum policies influence the classroom practices of teachers and learning experiences of children. He has been invited to speak nationally and internationally and has presented his work at numerous professional meetings and conferences. His most recent book, *Holding Schools Accountable: A Handbook for Educators and Parents*, offers parents and teachers straightforward information about current accountability policies and offers them clear advise about ways to demand accountability policies that lead to genuine improvements in educational quality and equity. He is also an assistant editor for the *Journal of Curriculum and Pedagogy*, the journal of the Curriculum and Pedagogy Group.

Sandra Stewart is an assistant professor at Stephen F. Austin State University in the Department of Secondary Education and Educational Leadership. Stewart spent seventeen years in public education as a teacher, administrative assistant, and principal. She earned an M.A. in educational leadership in 1997 and a doctorate in educational leadership in 2004. Her research interests include educational leadership, curriculum and instruction, educational reform, and social justice issues.

Kimberley A. Woo is an assistant professor of education at Cal State San Marcos in San Marcos, California. She has been working with the teaching and learning faculty group to prepare K–6 classroom educators. Woo has authored a number of scholarly publications including *Asian American Preservice Candidates: A Snapshot of Attitude Toward the Field, Growing Up Asian in America: The Role of Social Context and Education in Shaping Racial and Personal Identity Research Interests Focus on Asian American Students,* and *"Double Happiness," Double Jeopardy: Exploring Ways in Which Race/Ethnicity and Gender Influence Self-Perceptions in Chinese American High School Girls.* Woo's research interests include Asian American students, multicultural education, and teacher preparation. Woo hopes her work will accomplish three objectives: to decrease the chasm between theory and practice and increase the dialogue among students, classroom teachers, and university professors; to promote awareness of multiculturalism by developing, organizing, and facilitating ongoing discussions focused on issues of diversity; and to incorporate Asian and Pacific American experiences into more complete philosophical and historical frameworks.

9 781607 091073